Not Just  r Swan

The life of dancer Silvia Ebert

As told to Angela Wigglesworth

Published by New Generation Publishing in 2018

Copyright © Angela Wigglesworth 2018

First Edition

My thanks to The Telegraph for permission to use the
photographs of The Ebert Family (p73) and
The Family Tree (p.74).

Front cover: Silvia adjusts her ballet shoe before the first
performance of the 1953 London Palladium production
of *Cinderella.*

www.newgeneration-publishing.com

Books by the same author:

Falkland People (Peter Owen)
People of Scilly (Sutton)
People of Wight (Sutton)
Lewes, A Photographic History of Your Town. (Francis Frith publications)
The Chair Man (New Generation Publishing)

Acknowledgements

I would like to thank David Arscott, Ann Cullen, Guy Earl and Leo Nasskau for their meticulous proof reading, Tony Tree for his help with the photographs and his picture of Silvia (p.119), and Chris Wigglesworth for giving me so much of his time and the benefit of his IT skills.

I would like to thank Julia Aries, Glyndebourne Archivist for her invaluable help providing me with information about Silvia's performances at Glyndebourne, and to Jim Ring for the use of his DVD: Ashmoles at High and Over.

Silvia and her opera director husband Peter Ebert, behind the curtain during the production of 'Idomeneo' at Glyndebourne in 1952.

*For Peter and my beautiful family who have made my life
such a joy*

CONTENTS

Chapter 1

My family

My sister, Stella, was three when I was born on July 31, 1926 and I was meant to be a boy to carry on the family name – I think my mother always wished I had been. My parents were living in Rome but when I was due to be born my mother went back to England, to Eastbourne where my grandmother lived, so I would be English, this little boy, who turned out to be me, a girl. It was in the middle of the General Strike – students were driving the trains and Mussolini was in power. Instead of being born in Rome, it was Eastbourne. I've always thought it was a bit of a comedown.

My mother's family were landed gentry of Swiss stock. Before the First World War, the name was von Peyer but they changed it to 'de Peyer' to make it more acceptable in England. I think they got the 'de' from an ancestor who became famous for discovering patches on the intestines and these are still called *Peyer Patches*. The family has three branches: the English one (because my grandfather came to England and married this English woman, my grandmother), a branch in Geneva and one in Schaffhausen, both in Switzerland.

My mother, Dorothy, lived in a grand Victorian house covered with ivy in Newent, Gloucestershire. When she was growing up the family had a Polish nanny, Miss Fenski, and my mother and her siblings lived in the nursery under her rule. Never seen or heard. Later, Miss Fenski used to come and stay with us and was a presence in my childhood too, but she couldn't stand the wind and it was always windy at High and Over, our house in Buckinghamshire. One of my memories of her is how she used to get out all the sheets and mend them and when my sister, Stella, had her first baby, she came back to look after her.

My mother had three brothers and two sisters, but only the boys counted. And only the boys inherited. This was a cause of enormous resentment to my mother all her life, though I must say one of the brothers, Charles, was nice and lent her money when she and my father, Bernard, came to build High and Over. I think they were in debt to him all their lives. Of the three brothers, (Charles, Eric and Esme), one was nice, one not nice, one sort of OK.

My uncle Charles, the one I liked, was a lovely way-out character, very socialist, and embarrassed at having a lot of money. But he married an American girl who loved it – she liked pretty clothes and they had a very expensive penthouse flat in Portland Place in London, and a country house. But they weren't happy and she went off to America with their daughter. He was in the European Coal and Steel Community and very politically involved – he always said he was one of the founders of the Common Market. Eric, the youngest, was quite nice, but never achieved anything very much. In his old age, he took up the Alexander Technique and taught it. Esme, the adored eldest son, was terribly spoilt. He never had a career but fancied himself a singer.

The three girls were Hilda, Christine and my mother. Hilda and Christine weren't allowed to go to university – their father didn't think it was any use – and they never married. But when he died, Hilda, who had polio as a child that had left her with rather a deformed face, took school-leaving exams, and went to university to study medicine. She became a psychiatrist and qualified when she was in her thirties. She was a lovely woman, very intelligent and sympathetic. Christine was a kind of missionary in Khartoum and a headmistress. She was very strict. The story I like best about her is when she was at a school in

India, she took her girls for an outing. They were all trained never to have to pee when they were out, but she needed to. So she made them make a circle around her and turn their backs so she could go.

The Swiss side of the family are still in touch and hold gatherings every five years but until recently the girls were never invited. My mother was always furious about this and when all the boys had died, she made such a fuss that one of the younger generation said 'OK, let's invite Dorothy.' By that time, she was very old and couldn't go but we, her children, did. We had another family gathering last year in Bath. They are very lavish affairs – the family have a lot of money.

My mother wasn't a warm person, rather cool. I think the children were all a bit frightened of her, a bit in awe. She wasn't a cuddly kind of mother but she was always very good to me. When I was a teenager, my shoulder blades stuck out and she thought if I lay on my back on the floor every day, it would help. She used to read to me: *Lorna Doone*, Dickens and the classics. She had good taste in literature but she hadn't been to university and had a chip on her shoulder about this. Bernard's friends were mostly academic and I think she always felt rather left out, especially when they lived in Oxford with all the North Oxford blue-stockings.

I feel she couldn't have been very good at socialising; when we were living in Amersham she never made any friends. But she was a very good wife and a very good cook, which she learnt to be in the First World War when she was in the VAD (Voluntary Aid Detachment) – a voluntary unit of civilians who worked in field hospitals and places of recuperation back in Britain.

My maiden name was Ashmole and my father, Bernard, followed in the steps of his ancestor, Elias Ashmole. He was not a direct ancestor because he (Elias) had no children; maybe the line was from an uncle. Elias Ashmole lived in the 17th century and collected astrological, medical and historical manuscripts, which he donated to Oxford University to create the Ashmolean Museum.

Bernard – we always called him 'Bernard' not 'father' – was born in Ilford in Essex in 1884, and his father was a director of the then new Ilford film company. It was like Kodak, they made little rolled films. Bernard was the baby of the family of five children: Constance, the oldest, was eighteen years older than him. Then there was Gladys, a physiotherapist and masseuse. She never married and travelled all over the world, a very enterprising lady. She lived with us in Amersham during the war, treating wounded soldiers in the local hospital. Muriel died, I don't know how. Gordon was an engineer and married Dot – she and her mother had a chicken farm in Devon – and he was involved in the floating Mulberry Harbours in the Second World War. He was incredibly boring. Later in life, when he and Bernard met, which they hardly ever did, Bernard would say, 'hello, old man,' and Gordon would say 'hello, old man' and that was it.

In the First World War, Bernard was awarded the MC for rescuing wounded soldiers under fire when everyone else from the trenches had gone into hiding. Nearly all his regiment perished in France but he survived and I think he always had a guilt feeling about this. It was in France at that time, that he bought the large round table that I still have. It had seven layers of paint on it which he stripped off – it was already an antique when he bought it.

He couldn't return to the war, he had a lot of shrapnel in his leg, and was very lame; he was never able to play tennis or any sports again. I think he was vaguely related to my mother and was convalescing in Newent Court, the grand country house where she lived, when they met. He

4

proposed in the Peach House, very romantic. Peter, my husband, and I visited it one day. The house had gone but I talked to the people in the local library. 'Oh yes,' they said, 'the manor house used to employ everyone in the village.'

My parents got married after the war and lived in Oxford where he was an archaeology lecturer. He must have studied there as a student before the war and Oxford, he always said, was a very sad place then, so many killed. He was very young to be chosen to be director of the British School of Art in Rome, but the two professors running it were quarrelling all the time and Bernard was appointed to take their place. Although young, he was a very practical and enterprising person and turned the school around – improved the heating system, made the food better and allowed students to have boy or girl friends. It was when Barbara Hepworth, John Skeaping and Rex Whistler were there and I think my parents had a marvellous time.

After I was born, my parents went back to Rome and Bernard and Amyas Connell, a New Zealand architectural student at the British School in Rome, designed a house for when they would return to England. They looked for the ideal plot of land and found a bare, flinty hillside above the village of Amersham in Buckinghamshire which they thought was right. They called the house High and Over, the name suggested by my mother from a hillside near Alfriston in Sussex.

I was three when they came back to England in 1930. Mussolini was in power and they wanted me to be English, they said, and not turned into a little Italian Fascist. In 1939, Bernard became keeper of the Greek and Roman antiquities in the British Museum, and professor of archaeology at London University, holding both jobs at the same time. He had incredible vibes for sculpture and had his own cast gallery in University College. He was one of the first people to teach archaeology from sculpture casts. He'd say you have to be able to see sculpture in the round.

Before the Second World War, he had the mammoth task of packing up the Elgin marbles, thousands of pieces, to store in the tunnels under the Aldwych tube station – it was the deepest unused one in London. He was always involved in discussions about the marbles and some of them, he said, would still be at the bottom of the sea if Elgin hadn't fished them out.

When Mr Getty was opening his museum on the west coast of California, he asked Bernard, who had retired and was in his seventies or eighties, to travel around Europe visiting the museums of the world at Mr Getty's expense, to buy sculptures for the museum. He and my mother had a wonderful time choosing them. But neither Mr Getty nor Bernard ever saw the museum because they were both so old and didn't want to fly. When Peter and I visited it years later, the curator showed us round and said: 'this was Bernard's', 'that was Bernard's'. Even when Bernard was really old they tried to persuade him to fly to America to decide whether a piece of sculpture was real or fake. In recent years it has become a big thing to sell off fakes to museums.

In the Second World War and in his forties, Bernard joined the RAF and was adjutant of a squadron. The Germans were coming down through Greece and he thought he might be able to help because he knew the country so well. He decided the squadron would have to evacuate and knew of a bay where they could bring in a ship to rescue the men. He hired a train, took the men there, got them off in time and was awarded the Greek Flying Cross. He went to Iraq and then out to the Far East where he was evacuated from Singapore when the Japanese invaded. He was in Mountbatten's headquarters in Delhi until the end of the

6

war – he used to say Mountbatten was quite a ladies' man and I don't think he really approved of him.

Chapter 2

High and Over. Philip. Home schooling. Holidays.
Childhood days.

High and Over

High and Over was a lovely white house based on a
hexagon, with about seven acres of land. Bernard had
trouble getting planning permission to build it. The
planning authority disliked the house but there was
nothing about it that they could legally object to and they
had to pass the plans. But when Bernard said he wanted to
have a swimming pool and fountains, the local council
said sorry, if he wanted so much water, he'd have to build
his own water tower, which he did. The planning
application was turned down but Bernard persisted and the
council finally passed it though, they said, 'with great
reluctance'. The tower was built with a spiral staircase in a
column leading up to a big drum at the top that contained
the water. Stella and I each had a little garden of our own
built on the flat roof of the house and we had a sand pit,
rings for gymnastics and bunk beds where we slept out in
the summer. We used to paint and draw there.

High and Over was an iconic building, criticised and

praised in the press. *Country Life* magazine sent an architect to review it. *Pathé News* made a film about it called The Dream House.

Bernard and our gardener, George, laid out the garden themselves. Gardening was Bernard's passion but he had terrible hay fever and suffered with it all summer. One of my earliest memories is going round the garden with him and he pulled up a little carrot, washed it under the tap and gave it to me, and then going into the greenhouse and smelling the tomatoes. I was about four. He had very high ideals, was very highly principled and had a lovely sense of humour. His family were a little bit puritan and Peter always said I had a puritan streak.

I think Bernard may have met George when he was in the army. When we moved to High and Over, George and his wife, May, came with us and Bernard had a lodge built for them in our drive. George was an interesting man – he taught himself to play the violin and had a collection of classical records. He was quite a gloomy man and only ever seemed happy when something was wrong. He didn't like to talk to my mother. He belonged to Bernard. May used to do what they called the rough cleaning and would come up to the house to wash floors. She did all the laundry, too. She had a heart of gold – I remember she made me a wonderful cake for my twenty first birthday. We also had a cook and a housekeeper. George and May were both very loyal and when, many years later, my parents moved from High and Over to Iffley near Oxford, they (my parents) bought them a house nearby. Their friendship lasted over fifty years.

There was a vast expanse of lawn at High and Over and Bernard decided to buy a roller. He bought a second-hand motor mower with roller attached that turned out to be a hand mower and had been converted to a motor one by fitting a motor cycle engine to it with a cycle chain. One day, George had rolled a great part of the lawn when the sprocket wheel caught in his overall, then into his trousers, tore into his leg and severed the main artery. Bernard was standing by the window in his study when he saw this happening.

He rushed down to the garage and seized the first thing that came to hand – a bundle of electric flex – and made a double tourniquet high up round George's thigh, using the starting handle of the mower as a lever, twisting it tightly round the leg to stop the bleeding. When the doctor came he said George would have died within six minutes if Bernard hadn't acted the way he did. Having been in the First World War, he had been trained for that sort of thing and he saved George's life. I think the hospital tried to save his leg but had to amputate it. George never liked his artificial one but managed well on crutches. He always sat on the ground when doing a gardening job like sowing or transplanting seedlings.

Bernard got his swimming pool. At the time, he was working in London as Keeper of the Greek and Roman antiquities at the British Museum and Professor of archaeology at London University, and every evening he'd come home and he and George would dig out the round pool: sixty barrow loads of earth a day and all by hand. It was shallow at the edges, six feet in the middle, with a flight of steps leading down to it and cypress trees on both sides. The soil was clay and flint, great for fruit trees, and we had lots of them – apples, pears, cherries, plums, peaches and figs. Part of our land was rented out to a farmer who had cows, but much of it was a vegetable garden, so we had lots of fresh vegetables. No junk food. This was an absolute saviour in the war.

Silvia, aged twelve, in the rose garden

Bernard was a lovely father. My memories of my childhood and doing fun things were mostly with him. He thought we could fly and we'd run down the very steep hill in the garden holding a tarpaulin behind us, but we never took off. He'd make a bonfire and cook potatoes. They were always hard and smoky but lovely. He was very sweet with us and very keen we should have high ideals. And principles. You couldn't lie to him. 'A lie is an attempt to deceive,' he'd say. He was absolutely straight and expected you to be too.

I had a very happy childhood. When I was five I went to the local school for a short while and remember one little girl doing a puddle on the floor, and another finding it difficult to read, staggering over every word. I could read fluently by then – my sister Stella was very keen on reading and had taught me when I was three because I kept disturbing her. My parents didn't feel the school was up to scratch and decided they would have a little school at High and Over for us, and two daughters of our neighbours who were about the same age.

Our governess was called Margaret Pearson. She had a dramatic first day – my brother, Philip, was born unexpectedly, and my mother had delivered him herself on her bedroom floor before the nurse coming to look after her arrived. My mother was walking round the outside of the house and had struck her head against some scaffolding. The shock apparently hastened the birth. Years later, I remember my mother standing in my kitchen and saying, 'Then I got my boy'. Not very sensitive of her. Many years after, when Philip's wife had a baby, my mother rang me and said: 'It's a disaster, it's a girl'.

I think I learnt my mothering skills on Philip. He was seven years younger than me and I loved him and looked after him. If there was any problem with him, I had to step in and help. He is now an ornithologist and lives in Peebles. He became a professor at Yale and at Edinburgh universities and when he retired, he managed to negotiate an agreement for a large part of the Scottish border to be planted with indigenous trees. I think it now belongs to the Woodland Trust. He has lectured in America and Edinburgh and, with his wife, Myrtle, has recently brought out a book on the Canaries.

Margaret Pearson was lovely. Small, petite, absolutely excellent. I can still remember our French and Italian lessons, and the prayers and hymns she liked. I could recite them all today. My cousin, Gillian, joined the class – Gillian was staying with us at the time because her parents were living in India and didn't think the climate suitable for children. She was a very one-off character, eighteen months younger than me; I was her best friend but she never uttered a word to my mother, she was so shy. She was meant to go and stay every now and then with her granny, Constance, my father's older sister, but Bernard's family were so spaced out in age that her granny was my aunt. Different generation. She didn't want to go and would spend the previous evening under her bed in floods of tears and my poor parents had to somehow get her there.

Our days were very structured: breakfast, lessons, lunch, more lessons and a walk. We had a cook and a housemaid and a lovely modern kitchen. In the morning, my mother would go to the kitchen and have a discussion with the cook. There was a table at one end where she (the cook) and the maid would eat. At the other end there were two sinks, one for cutlery and a teak one for china so it didn't get scratched. There was even a built-in fridge, very unusual in those days. At meal times, my mother had a bell under the table and we could always see her trying to find this with her foot if the table had been moved a bit. She would ring and the maid would come in. It was in the 1930s but by the end of the war people didn't have servants.

In the holidays, we children used to go and stay with our granny in Eastbourne. It was a big ritual: we'd be up in the nursery and at the first gong we'd go and wash our hands. At the second, we'd go down and there was this enormous table, with miles between each person and each with their own cruet set. There was a long sideboard with little maids standing each end, and at breakfast there was a stand with a dish for the cornflakes and an electric fire to make them crisp. There were oval-shaped silver dishes with lids and there'd be eggs and bacon, sausages, kidneys, sardines on toast. I don't think the little maids were there at breakfast, I think we helped ourselves, but they were there at other meals and heard all our conversation. I thought that was rather weird.

We weren't nervous but we had to behave. I didn't like fish and would store it in my cheek, then eat my pudding with the fish still there. We always had to go to church with granny, and Stella used to say I'd put on my church face. I played the role of good little girl. When I went to stay there with my nanny, Miss Fenski, to convalesce after I'd had my tonsils out, I had a lovely time. I was in a double room with a little red-haired boy and we had such fun. I must have been very frail because I remember being in a pushchair and I was six.

We were encouraged to read a lot. My mother used to read aloud to us after lunch: she liked Jane Austen, the Brontes and *The Swiss Family Robinson*. On Sunday mornings we used to go into my parents' bed and Bernard would read *Strange Stories from a Chinese Studio*. I had no idea what it was or why I remember it but now I realise it was a very famous book. Everyone was very formal: we children didn't stay up for dinner. We had Ovaltine and an orange brought upstairs in a lift from the kitchen to the nursery that was on the top floor. We had our own bathroom up there and a room for a nanny or a governess. Quite posh, really.

We didn't see our parents much but I remember their dinner parties. When I couldn't sleep at night, I'd go down in my little nightie. I don't think they liked that – they had all these intellectuals and visiting professors from America. But when we had lunch with them, we were always encouraged to take part in the conversation, to put our spoke in and to listen. My Uncle Charles, the Socialist one, would have political conversations with them and awful arguments which I hated. My mother was very Conservative and I think Bernard rather let her get on with it. I always thought it was going to lead to divorce. I hated that whole concept but later thought it was good to encourage us, very different from the 'children should be seen and not heard' custom at the time.

My parents were Church of England but slack about going to church. We were very isolated up there on the hill; they didn't have a car and walked everywhere. The nearest church was in Amersham where they occasionally went for communion, but they didn't like the clergy. So, Stella, Gillian and I were sent off on our bikes on our own to Chesham Bois the next village, which was too far for my parents to walk. We had a penny each for the collection and used to save them to buy a gobstopper each on the way home. These changed colour when you sucked them, and we kept taking them out of our mouths to see what colour they were.

Then our governess had a disaster in her family and had to leave. Her brother had died of blood poisoning, a nail had damaged his foot. Our second governess wasn't so good and we had different children sharing lessons. Having a governess meant we didn't have the social life of a school, so it was good that our parents and Gillian's decided we should go to boarding school.

Chapter 3

Stella. Quaker boarding school.
Cheltenham Ladies' College.

Stella wasn't happy at boarding school so she lived with our granny in Eastbourne and went to Moira House, a day school that I think is still there today. It was very strong in English but had no science. When she decided she wanted to be a doctor, she went to a school in Bournemouth and stayed with our aunt. She had to do all the science subjects from scratch but she did really well and became head girl.

In fact, she did become a doctor. She went to university during the war and fell in love with an extremely glamorous and brilliant student, Peter, who came from an East End London family. My poor mother, on her own because Bernard was away in the RAF in the Far East, had to decide whether Stella should be allowed to marry him because both parents thought it was not acceptable they should live together. They did marry, they were very much in love, and had four children. Peter became one of the leading surgeons for pioneering hip transplants – if you had your hip done by him, it was something. But he left my sister and married a nurse. It was terrible for Stella. She was a very sensitive person.

I didn't mind being away from home at all. We went to a Quaker school in Wendover in Buckinghamshire, very small, not more than a hundred girls – I think most schools were same sex at that time – with a lovely atmosphere. It was a farm school with lots of animals and Gillian was very keen on animals too, we'd both been riding before. At the beginning of term, each child was allocated an animal – every department had one or two older girls, some 13-year-olds, and some little ones. Rabbits and chickens were for the smaller children, and stable work, cows and pigs were for the older girls. I helped look after the goats. My favourite was rather an elderly lady and very difficult to milk: someone had to hold her back legs so she wouldn't kick. She had a darling little kid and one day I was told that the kid was old enough to be tethered. So I tethered it and when I came out later, it had strangled itself. It was awful. Terrible. But I'd been told to do it. I still remember how upset I was. It makes me cry now, all these years later. They just did it too young – it was a scarring experience. I can still feel it.

The headmistress was a biology teacher and really excellent. All the school would have assembly in her study and everyone sat on the floor – it must have been a big room and I remember there was a fireplace; she'd read a passage from a book and then we sat in silence for a quarter of an hour. The period was called Recollections – we had to think about what she'd read. I don't remember the books, but obviously they were thought-provoking. A quarter of an hour seemed quite a long time.

The school was a big success but they didn't have classics which my parents had wanted me to do, and I was taken away. I had got on very far in the biology class and was dissecting frogs before I left. When I went on to my next school and told them about this, they were astonished I was doing it at that age. I think I would have become a doctor if I'd stayed at the Quaker school

* * * * * * *

It was 1939, the beginning of the Second World War, I was thirteen and we were all at different schools. Stella was at the Talbot Heath High day school in Bournemouth, Philip went to Bryanston, and I went to Cheltenham Ladies' College.
The government had taken over the Cheltenham College

17

buildings, and we were evacuated with whichever boarding house we were already in. I was sent to Lilleshall Hall in Shropshire. But I didn't go with the lovely house mistress, Miss Truesdale, my mother had chosen and who was interested in the arts, but to another house with army huts and cast iron stoves. It was freezing in winter and run by two awful women – we just didn't like each other. I had been such a good little girl before this, my parents couldn't understand what had happened, but those teachers did bring out the worst in me.

The food was disgusting. I remember being sent out because I couldn't eat macaroni pudding. They used to cook with peanut butter, say for a roly-poly pudding, and I didn't like suet puddings. At teatime we had just bread and a scraping of jam. Sweets were rationed. I remember, by the end of the war, we had tuppence every week to spend on a little bar of chocolate. We used to knit gloves and balaclavas for the RAF – I was very aware of the war because Bernard was away.

But then the government decided they needed the buildings we'd been evacuated to, so we left that ghastly place and went back to Cheltenham. My mother was able to move me to a different house just outside the town and we were bussed-in for lessons.

Cheltenham College was rather philistine – hardly anything in the way of arts, but there was music. I learnt the violin and played in the school orchestra but I don't think I chose the instrument. It was chosen for me. Now I realise it's much better to start children on a wind instrument. Strings are difficult. We had to do the science stream or classics. I was very well on in science but my parents wanted me to do classics and I had to change. I was very resentful. How could they do that to me? My mother, quite rightly I expect, thought I would be lazy unless I was pushed, and there was a class for bright children. She got me moved up and I did have to work a bit harder, starting from scratch with Greek and Latin. There were only three of us doing it and it was tough. I wasn't very well there – coughs and colds. Wartime food, I expect. Babies all qualified for orange juice and dried milk, and at the end of the war they were healthier than they'd ever been. We kept chickens at High and Over and a real egg put in with a dried one made it much better.

Miss Popham was the headmistress and my mother told me she'd sent me there because that was where she and her sisters had been. They'd had a marvellous headmistress called Miss Faithfull who taught bible study, but Miss Popham wasn't marvellous. The story is that Miss Faithfull asked Miss Popham what her interests were and she said, 'classics and dogs', and Miss Faithfull said, 'My dear, for a woman in your position that is a very disgraceful admission!'

Chapter 4

War years, 1939 to 1945. My mother and I run High and Over. Guests from bombed cities. Harrods' delivery van. The Cone Ripman School of Dancing. Doodlebugs. Dancing school life.

Because High and Over was such a big house with a big garden, lots of our relatives and friends during the Second World War wanted to come and live with us – we were 'north of London' and therefore considered safer from the bombing than the south- coast areas.

We had Sir George Hill, director of the British Museum, a lovely, intelligent man who smoked cigars so everything smelt of them, our aunt, Gladys, the physiotherapist, who was allocated to the Amersham military hospital to treat wounded soldiers. I think she got on my mother's wick sometimes. An actress from the Amersham Rep was billeted on us and at one time we had a family with four children from the East End of London. But they didn't like being on top of a hill – they couldn't pop out to buy a bun for the children's lunch – and they soon left. My granny from Eastbourne was there because they didn't think Eastbourne was a safe place. She came with her companion who was a vegetarian, so we always had to have something for her.

We had no active men around, they'd all been called up. I was really the man of the house and had to cope if there was a crisis. I think my mother and I must have got close. After having had servants all her life – they were now called up – she had to cook for all these people. We were lucky with the catering because food rationing, which was very strict towards the end of the war, was not so bad for a big family with a well-stocked vegetable garden. My mother once tried to put some of our sugar ration aside to make jam when the fruit ripened. There were tears when Bernard, home on leave, unwittingly used it to experiment with making cherry wine. We had a few children there so they were supplied with the dried egg stuff that the Americans sent us, dried milk, rather horrible, concentrated orange juice and cod liver oil. Rationing continued long after the war ended when Germany was already being supplied by America. We cooked very healthy food with lots of vegetables and salads and very little was fried.

The only help we had was from George and May. My mother and I fed all these people and, being so remote, everything was delivered even though we had petrol rationing. The baker came, the butcher came. What really impressed me was that Harrods had this enormous green delivery van and it came every week all through the war to bring my mother's library books. She belonged to their lending library.

Sometimes in the holidays, my mother and I would have a day in London and once we went to see the ballet, *Les Sylphides,* at The New Theatre. It might have been soon after that when I was making a bed in one of the rooms at High and Over, that I thought I had to be a ballet dancer; my parents always played records and I could hear classical music on the radio. I had an idea that my mother would like to have been a dancer herself or she may have picked up vibes from me otherwise I don't think she would have taken the action she did if Bernard had not been away. To her Victorian father, the idea of the stage for his daughter would have been a fate worse than death though her family was very musical. My grandmother was a founder member of Glyndebourne opera house and my oldest Uncle Esme's son was Gervase de Peyer, the clarinettist.

21

It was a difficult decision for her to let me leave Cheltenham after I'd taken School Certificate, the equivalent of today's GCSE, to become a dancer. She and Bernard couldn't really correspond properly, there were those blue aerogrammes and it took forever to get an answer. So my mother had to decide whether to take me away and let me start dancing, or make me stay on with a lot of pressure from the school, as there would probably have been from Bernard if he'd been there. She took the decision to let me leave and I did take School Certificate first in case a ballet career didn't work out. My teacher, Miss Truesdale, was lovely about it. When I said I wanted to go, she said, 'Well, it's a bit late to start dancing but have fun.' Years later when I was dancing with Glyndebourne in the Edinburgh Festival – I was in the brothel scene in *The Rake's Progress* – she came to see me.

My mother found someone locally to vet me and see if my limbs were loose enough to become a dancer. It seems I was alright and they chose the Ripman School of Dancing in London run by Olive Ripman. This had amalgamated with the Cone School of Dancing that had moved out of London to Tring in the war and later became the Arts Educational School, now known as Arts Ed.

I was sixteen in 1941 when I started at Mrs Ripman's. It was in Baker Street and Olive Ripman was a lovely woman. She had all the right ideas – small classes and guest teachers. It was basically modern dance, Greek, ballroom and there were excellent ballet teachers. I didn't like tap but did well at all the other things – musical comedy, ballroom, Greek. I liked ballet most.

I commuted every day from High and Over all through the doodlebug raids. It was quite a scary time. The doodlebugs were coming over and when you heard the engine stop you knew it was coming down. I was once on Baker Street station when it came very close. Mrs Ripman was a bit oblivious about the war and we always had our modern dance sessions in a studio with a glass roof. I think it was only me and another girl who were having a lesson with a lovely ancient pianist playing the grand piano, when a doodlebug came over and we all dived under the piano, the pianist, Mrs Ripman, the other girl and me, until the doodlebug had landed. Many children left the school and I had almost personal tuition. There were quite a few people there who later became well-known: Gillian Lynne who choreographed *Cats*, John Gilpin who went on to the Festival Ballet and Moira Fraser who was in the Royal Ballet. I was a total beginner but I cottoned on quite quickly and worked like crazy. I knew this was what I wanted to do but I think my whole career was more about feeling than technique.

Mrs Ripman had advertised the school as giving a full-time education but of course there were hardly any teachers. I was allocated to teach Art – at 16! Lana Morris came to the class and went on to become a starlet. I really enjoyed it. I think I was fatalistic about the bombing.

Sometimes I had to come home late at night and High and Over was a marker, this big white house on the top of a hill, for the English and Germans. The Home Guard had a look out post at the top of the water tower and when I was late getting back, a guard would be crawling about among the bushes, shouting 'Who goes there?' And I'd say, 'it's alright, I'm only going to the house.'

Chapter 5

*London life. Earl's Court flat. First job. My dancing
career begins. Noel Coward's Revue. Touring.
Theatrical digs. I audition for the Royal Ballet*

I'd been wanting to rent a flat in London because the
commuting was a bit much but I was quite young to rent
on my own. I think my mother was keen I should be with
someone and we learned that one of the teachers at the
school, Sheila Nicholson, wanted to find a flat, part-time,
in London. She taught in the country as well, and was only
in London a couple of days a week. She asked me if I
would like to share a flat with her and we found one in
Earl's Court – it was the grottiest area. Terrible. The odd
thing was that my mother never came to meet Sheila or
look at the flat before I moved in. She could have been
anybody. The flat was overlooking the railway line and we
couldn't talk when a train was passing. But Sheila and I
got on well – she was rather a tease. She liked to attract
men, string them along, then drop them. I didn't really
approve and she got herself into a real fix. She become
engaged to a guy who was in the colonial service and gone
out to Nigeria, and she'd promised to marry him when he
came back. In the meantime, she had quite a hot kind of
love affair with a French guy who used to come over from
Paris and stay in our flat. He was lovely. But then the other
guy came home from Nigeria and Sheila said that, as she'd
promised to marry him, she would. I said, 'but Sheila, you
can't do it, it's not right.' She did marry him. It was an
awful marriage.

I was at Mrs Ripman's when I got my first job. It was in
Noel Coward's intimate revue called *Sigh No More* at the
Piccadilly Theatre. Sheila was the choreographer for one
of the numbers and had recommended me. It was very

exciting. How lucky can you be to go straight into a West End show?

It was 1945 and I was nineteen. It was the beginning of my career.

Dancing days

Today, many people don't know what an intimate revue is, but Coward's music was a typical example of the witty numbers that made up the show. In between songs they needed something else and brought on the dancers. In *Sigh No More* there were twelve of us and one of the numbers was based on *Blithe Spirit*. There were three Elviras and three Ruths and I was one of the Elviras. One song, *Nina from Argentina*, with a lot of Spanish dancing in the background, was very popular. Madge Elliot and Cyril Richard, a married couple and musical comedy stars, were in it. Madge wanted to do a dance number but she was really past it – she'd been a musical comedy star before the war. But Coward let them do it and when Cyril Richard got her up on his shoulder, and she was lying there as part of the dance routine, and said the now famous: 'Very flat, Norfolk', it sort of sent them up and made it alright. Cyril got ill quite soon after we opened in London and Coward didn't want to risk the show, so sang one of the songs himself. In the very romantic *Matelot, Matelot* song, we dancers came on in a kind of dream sequence when a sailor was thinking about his girl friend and I was the innocent, romantic young girl.

Coward had written that song specially for Graham Payn, a young tenor, who went on to become Coward's permanent partner. He had also written a song with different styles of music and Graham Payn danced with each of us in turn. We had costumes modelled for us by Jacqmar, a top West End designer, and were measured up for dresses that were meant to match our personalities. But when they saw them on the stage they didn't like them, and produced other dresses, almost all the same. Mine was pale green chiffon with yellow underneath and very pretty.

Joyce Grenfell was also in *Sigh No More* – I think it was her first professional part. She was rather looked down on in the theatre world as being a drawing-room entertainer, but she was the hit of the show. Vivien Merchant, later an actress, was in it too. She was a very cool dancer and went on to marry Harold Pinter. Sadly, she later committed suicide.

Sigh No More opened in the Manchester Opera House in July 1945 and transferred to London at The Piccadilly Theatre in August. But first it went on tour. Theatrical digs at that time were really ghastly. My parents came up for my first night and I stayed with them at the Queen's Hotel, a posh hotel. After they left, we had three weeks in Manchester and I moved into digs with another dancer. It was awful. We had breakfast and supper after the show with our landlady and the food was disgusting. The loo paper was the telephone directory. There was an old-fashioned flat-iron we had to put on the gas and it scorched our clothes. We used to pass on digs' addresses to others – £2.50 a week, £3.50 for good ones. With *Sigh No More* we only went to Manchester and Liverpool, then down to London.

When I heard the show was closing, and the Royal Ballet was auditioning, I went along. Noel Coward was very nice about it and said, 'Yes, if you have the chance, take it.' He was a lovely man though very nervous and I could never understand why when he was such a star. I remember when I left and went to say goodbye, he was in Graham's dressing room. They didn't hide their relationship but there was no lovey-dovey.

I must have been nervous about the audition, but you are so confident when you're young, you think you can do anything and I was very ambitious. I wanted to be a classical dancer, but I should have understood I would never have been technically strong enough. And when I got into the ballet company, I realised you have no chance of expressing yourself because you have to be just like the next swan, for example, and in a way it's stultifying. You are in the hands of the choreographer and have to do what he or she says. I suppose it was quite disillusioning for me. I knew I was not technically up to it but Ninette de Valois,

27

who ran the company, said she could always tell a dancer from her first *pliés,* so I think I must have got in on that. I remember standing in a grotty telephone-box in Soho and ringing my parents and saying the best possible thing had happened. They were thrilled. All the time I was training at the Ripman School I was thinking the Royal Ballet was my highest ambition.

Chapter 6

The Royal Ballet (Sadler's Wells). Ballet classes.
Ninette de Valois. Margot Fonteyn, Frederick Ashton,
Beryl Grey, Moira Shearer. Ballet shoes.

Joining the company was a great moment. Well, it wasn't very nice, actually. We, the new ones, had rather a bad time because a lot of the older dancers in the established company had been through the whole slog of the war, and really didn't like these young girls coming in. They were rather horrible to us, bullying in a way, but we battled on.

The company wasn't known as the Royal Ballet then, it was Sadler's Wells and they were dancing at the New Theatre in St. Martin's Lane, I think it's now the Noel Coward Theatre. Ninette de Valois, who had started Sadler's Wells at the Old Vic, wanted to do ballet for the masses and not go to Covent Garden that she was then being asked to do. She didn't want to work with the snobs, she said, but to stay with 'the people' at the Old Vic. But she had to go to Covent Garden eventually and the company became the Royal Ballet. I remember Beryl Grey was one of their stars, she was really young, only 15. She was very tall and had enormous feet and when she was on points, there was hardly any man who could dance with her.

De Valois was small, neat and very strict, and I never saw her relax. She was a bit too rigid in her taste for me. She wanted everyone to conform to the English rather understated style of ballet and didn't like the Russian ballerina who came when I joined and had a very Russian carriage. In fact, de Valois was English and had studied in Russia, but took on the name because at that time you had to have a French name, like Margot. They all had foreign names.

In 1945, Covent Garden was going to re-open after the war – it had been a dance floor for the troops but now had been totally done up and refurbished. They were going to do a production of *Sleeping Beauty* with sets by Oliver Messel, and take on a few extra dancers.

At that time, we all went to ballet classes in studios near Cambridge Circus. It was a public class for anyone who didn't have anywhere to go for tuition – you could just pay your five shillings and go. There were two excellent ballet teachers – Vera Volkova and Anna Northcote. Volkova, a Russian teacher, was downstairs and Anna Northcote, an English teacher, was in the upstairs studio. You were either a Volkova or a Northcote girl. I went to Volkova's class. She was a fantastic teacher. It was at one of those ballet classes that Frederick Ashton, later well-known as a choreographer, said I should be in the Royal Ballet. I had just had an audition and I said: 'I am.' I remember he had tiny hands and feet and was a very dainty dancer.

Margot Fonteyn was there, and the Rambert daughters (Marie Rambert ran the Rambert Dance Company). Margot Fonteyn was very quiet, no star allure, but she had this lovely personality, this marvellous dancing quality. She had a kind of radiance. About thirty of us had to squash into a tiny dressing room, there was no shower or anything like that, just a loo and a wash basin. We were all hot and sweaty and Margot Fonteyn would leave looking a hundred dollars, groomed and beautiful. You couldn't imagine how she could do it. I was amazed when they said, in a film, that she had started so young because I always felt she had to struggle with her technique. Like the moment in *Sleeping Beauty* when she had to keep a pose and balance while being handed from one of four suitors to the next. You had to hold your breath and pray that it worked.

Moira Shearer was always fine. She had a very easy technique, very lovely and fluid. She'd been to a different type of ballet school, not so stiff. While I was there, she did the film, *The Red Shoes,* and I did camera tests for her. Ninette de Valois didn't like that. She thought Moira Shearer would bring the wrong public to Covent Garden! I thought she should have been glad to get an audience at all. William Chappell, another dancer was there, and Robert Helpmann.

It was very difficult to get ballet tights at this time. In fact, it was a nightmare. I had to knit my own and used darning wool because you could get that without clothes coupons. They say Margot Fonteyn only gave up dancing when she couldn't get her silk tights! We also had horrible cotton or rayon ones and you'd twist a penny in some tape to tighten them up – it was important not to have any creases. There was a great shortage of ballet shoes, too. Sometimes the points had worn right through to the floor and I was pirouetting on my toes. There were two or three ballet shoe makers in London and they'd make them specially for you. I had mine done at Freed's in Cecil Court, just off Charing Cross Road.

Chapter 7

*Sleeping Beauty, Covent Garden's first post-war
production. Queen Elizabeth (later, the Queen
Mother) and two princesses in the audience.
Anniversary performance fifty years later. I join an
American ballet company. On tour with 'Bullet in the
Ballet'. Landladies. A brothel. Ration books.*

The opening night of *Sleeping Beauty* at Covent Garden in
1945 was sensational. De Valois had been persuaded to
move there and there were three ballerinas doing the main
role: Margot Fonteyn, Moira Shearer, and Pamela May – I
was in the *corps de ballet,* and the Queen (later the Queen
Mother) was there with the two princesses. Fifty years on,
in 1995, there was an anniversary performance and
everyone who had been in the original cast was invited. I
was living in Italy at the time and happened to have a
friend staying who had brought somebody with him who
worked for the company. When she heard I had been in the
first production, she said I must come and she organised it.
I was given two tickets and took my daughter, Andrea. It
was very funny meeting all these people again. We had a
little rehearsal, and the idea was that at the end of the
performance, we would all line up on the stage and, one by
one, curtsy to the royal box and go to the side. Then a
child from the ballet school would come on and give the
Queen a flower. Darcey Bussell was in the ballet this time.

Because my professional name was Ashmole and started
with an 'A', I had to lead the dancers when the Queen
came on to the stage to meet Ninette de Valois who was
brought down in a wheel chair. She was in her 90s by then.
She and the Queen had difficulty understanding each other
and I had to act as interpreter. I think they just exchanged
pleasantries.

Back to 1945. We only did *Sleeping Beauty* that season, it was the only ballet there was. At the end of it, a selected company was chosen to go to New York for the first time, but I wasn't included. It was just the top dancers and they all got a new outfit, we were all so shabby after the war. I left the Royal Ballet and joined an American company that had come into Covent Garden. It was called The American Ballet Theatre and was terribly exciting because there was lots of modern ballet. I was there for a few months and we had a marvellous time with these Americans. Tall, lovely men and lots of talented people like Jerome Robbins and Michael Kidd who afterwards became top stars in America. We augmented the *corps de ballet* and danced in *Giselle*, *Petrushka* and one or two modern ballets. There were only a few we could do on that stage and the rest of the time we just went out front and watched. We hadn't seen anything like it in England. And, of course, the Americans weren't going to put up with the horrible food we were having so they took us to the poshest hotels and fed us with steaks. We had a very good time.

After that, I joined a company run by Jay Pomeroy who was putting on a show by Carol Brahms and S.J. Simon based on a book they'd written called *Bullet in the Ballet*. Leonide Massine, the choreographer, had brought over three male dancers from Paris – there weren't any in England because of the war. I think the twelve girls in the show were mostly chosen for their appearance more than anything else. I remember once on tour, we all went to the Turkish baths because we had nothing to do in the afternoon. We swept in and the other ladies looked at us. We did have a towel round us, but it must have been rather unexpected for them.

It was 1946, we had to give our ration books to our landladies. Four of us had the address of a flat and I think several of the actors came too. It was one of those big flats like there were in Glasgow, with an awful, smelly bathroom on the staircase. We thought we were going to have separate rooms but all four of us dancers were in one. It was near the front door, so when the bell rang late at night, I thought, well, one of the actors had probably got locked out and I got up to open the door. It was not one of the actors. The landlady came out with a carving knife and started shouting at me and all I'd done was open the door. We were, we realised, in a brothel. In the morning, she chucked us out. I suppose she thought I'd found her out and was angry with me for answering the door.

But before chucking us out, she cut out the tea and sugar coupons from our ration books. They were little white squares, one for each week, and she took the whole month. So of course when we wanted to get new digs, new landladies said they were sorry but they couldn't take us without a ration book. It was a nightmare. We had a dreadful time there.

We toured all round the northern cities, but it wasn't a big success. It was a terribly expensive play to stage because they needed actors, dancers and an orchestra. In Blackpool, I remember playing to rather empty houses in the winter. Can you imagine anything worse? In the first act the main character gets shot, the bullet in the ballet, so we had to do a bit of the ballet at the beginning and a bit at the end. They took all these people on tour with the result that at the end of it they ran out of money and the play crashed before it got to London.

1947 was a dreadfully cold winter. *Bullet in the Ballet* had finished and I hadn't got a job. I went to three auditions in London and got accepted in all of them. One was a tiny revue with Hermione Gingold and Hermione Baddeley – two big stars of the time – and three dancers, one of whom had dropped out so they needed another. But you had to have long blonde hair. I had long hair but it wasn't blonde.

There wasn't much dancing and it was terribly trivial and boring, so I wasn't mad about being in that every night. I auditioned for something else which I can't remember, and then for Glyndebourne. The choreographer there picked twelve dancers, one of whom was me. There were only going to be nine performances and then I would be out of work again, but I felt Glyndebourne was a name and had a reputation. Going there I thought, would be worth it. It was a fateful decision.

Chapter 8

Carl Ebert, Glyndebourne's first artistic director.
Peter Ebert, his son, theatre administrator and opera
director.

Carl Ebert became Glyndebourne's first artistic director in 1934. He was born in Germany in 1887, his father a Polish count, Anton Potulicky, the second son of a long line of Polish aristocrats. His mother was Mary Collins, an Irish-American music student. They were madly in love and Mary became pregnant. But such was the shame of an illegitimate child, they didn't tell anyone and asked a childless couple, Herr and Frau Ebert, whom Anton had lodged with, if they would look after the baby. Seven years later, the Eberts formerly adopted Carl. He was to be known as Charles Ebert but at the outbreak of the First World War, he decided to change his first name to Carl.

He trained for two years to be a banker but in 1907 he got a free place at Max Reinhardt's School of Dramatic Art in Berlin where he fell in love with Lucie Splisgarth (Cissie) at a Berlin bus stop. It took him some time to pluck up courage to offer her his umbrella, and seven years before he could afford to marry her; he had been supporting the Eberts financially. He and Cissie had two children: Hidde, who became an actress, and Peter, an opera director and theatre administrator.

Carl was a well-known actor in the German theatre before he became an opera director. He and Cissie were divorced in 1923. The following year he married Gertrude Eck and Cissie married the conductor, Hans Oppenheim. They all remained on good terms for the rest of their lives, even going on holidays together.

In the early 1930s, Carl was invited by the Nazi, Hermann Goering, to take charge of the theatre scene in Berlin but he hated that regime and decided to leave the country. In 1933, he went to Switzerland and then on to Turkey where he worked as an opera director during the war and founded the National Theatre of Turkey.

In 1934, he was invited by John Christie, a wealthy landowner, and his wife Audrey, to start an opera company at Glyndebourne, John's home in Sussex. Carl thought this was a mad idea – how could a single person, even one with a great estate, have enough money to finance something like that? He was used to German theatre subsidies. But he found the Glyndebourne idea, and John Christie, a challenge and fell in love with the beauty of the Sussex countryside. In 1934, with the conductor, Fritz Busch, they became Glyndebourne's first director and conductor when the doors of its new theatre opened with *The Marriage of Figaro*.

The Times wrote: 'what he (Ebert) accomplished at Glyndebourne in collaboration with Fritz Busch as conductor, was to give a living demonstration that opera was a form of art and not, as English tradition for a couple of centuries believed, a vehicle for star singers against tattered scenery and rough-and-ready stage management.' It was a great success.

Glyndebourne closed during the Second World War, but opened again in 1947 with Gluck's *Orfeo* – Carl Ebert and Fritz Busch at the helm.

Peter (Carl and Cissie's son) was born in Germany in 1918, seven months before the end of the war. They had separated when Peter was six, and he'd spent his school days going from one parent to the other until they decided it would be better if he went to a boarding school. The one they chose was in Salem in southern Germany, a preparatory school that had been run by Kurt Hahn, who also left Germany in the 1930s to found Gordonstoun in Scotland. When Carl realised what was happening in Germany under the Nazi regime, he asked Peter, then 14, whether he would like to stay there or go to Gordonstoun. Peter had always refused to take part in the Hitler Youth exercises at school and decided he would like to leave – it was a big decision for a young boy to make. His elder sister, Hidde, who was just starting as an actress, decided to stay in Germany. She committed suicide at the end of the war and nobody really knew why – Carl always had a bad conscience that it was because of his marriage breaking up when she was eleven, or whether it was because she felt guilty that she'd stayed in Germany and had performed for Hitler. It was terrible for the family.

Peter was one of the first twelve boys at Gordonstoun; Prince Philip was there but two or three years younger. The school was very much finding its feet and was very character forming. The boys weren't allowed to talk to anyone on Sundays: they had to go for a walk on their own in silence. They built their own boat and learnt how to sail, going out in incredibly rough seas. Peter was very happy there. He spoke fluent English but always had a German accent. I loved it, it was more the music of the language that I think he kept.

When he left school, he was interested in the diplomatic service but that would have meant studying modern Greats at Oxford and he realised his father couldn't have afforded it. There was a family conference at Rules, a restaurant off Fleet Street in London, to talk about his future, with Carl and his second wife, Gertie, (Peter's mother), Cissie, and her second husband, Hans Oppenheimer. The Oppis, as we called them, had also left Germany in the 1930s and gone to Dartington Hall in Devonshire where Dorothy and Leonard Elmhirst had started an experiment in rural rejuvenation to improve health and life of people in country areas. There was a junior and a senior school and an arts complex, and Hans had been given the task of building up a music department.

Peter describes what happened at the family lunch at Rules in the book he wrote about his father: *In This Theatre of Man's Life.*

'My parents debated the issues until one of them suddenly said: "Peter, for God's sake say something." I was well known in the family for being rather quiet. Since the whole situation had arisen unexpectedly for me, I had not yet found an alternative professional interest. It was decided that banking experience would do no harm and there was a certain amount of justice in that because my father had started the same way. I became a volunteer clerk, an apprentice, at the well-known commercial bank of S. Japhet and Co, in London Wall. The experience was fascinating. I took out a student subscription for *The Times*, bought a hat and an umbrella and travelled from my digs in Ennismore Gardens, South Kensington to Moorgate every day. The idea was that I should spend, say, two or three months in every department to learn the trade properly. After eighteen months, I decided that banking was not for me.

'The Oppis happened to hear that a teacher at the Senior School at Dartington was about to start a small film unit to make classroom and documentary films. In a flash, I saw that the combination of the artistic and the technical might be the right choice for me. Working in the theatre had simply never occurred to me as an option although I was surrounded by it in the family. Perhaps there was a hidden psychological barrier in having a famous theatre man as a father. He had never hinted that it would make him happy if I chose a theatrical career. I lived with the Oppis and became a student cinematographer.'

It was when Peter was working at Dartington that he met his first wife Kitty, and they had two children: Tabitha and Judith. Strangely enough, I could have met Peter when I was in the Royal Ballet but I never did. He was doing some work there, making gaiters for dancers in one of the hunting scenes. Kitty was very skilled at making handbags that they sold to Fortnum and Mason.

When France fell, and after the evacuation of Dunkirk in 1940, there was a big panic because everyone thought the Germans were going to invade and I think if they had done that would have been the end of the war. The British Government decided that all Germans, whether refugees or suspected Nazi sympathisers, should be interned. Oppi, who was interned, had a friend called Siegfried Ochs who had a revolver in his case. He was Jewish and wanted to shoot himself if the Germans came. When they were packing their cases to go into internment, a British policeman was in the room. The poor guy didn't know what to do with the gun, to smuggle it in or smuggle it out!

Peter became a 'friendly enemy alien' and he, too, was interned. He was sent to a Butlin's holiday camp and then to North Devon where he met up with some of his old German school friends. The main problem in a camp like that was there was nothing for them to do, so they thought they'd open an Information Centre. They didn't have any information, but people came for help who had court cases pending. Peter and his friends made notes and took them to the camp commander to see if they could get something done. He later went to Shropshire and then to the Isle of Man where he worked as an orderly in a hospital. It must have been very hard for him, he was awful about any injuries or seeing blood. But a friend helped him and orderlies did get better treatment. He was released after thirteen months and worked in factories in London and later on the land.

After the war, the Allied Powers occupying Germany invited Carl to undertake a tour of the country and report on the state of the German theatre. Peter went with him and they flew from London to Bunde, an army base in Westphalia, in a military aircraft, benches facing each other down the two sides of the fuselage. They were civilians in the military set up, and could only stay in hotels requisitioned by the Forces. They had a jeep which, the driver told them, had been through the Battle of El Alamein.

Peter was in London when Rudi Bing, first Managing Director of the Glyndebourne and Edinburgh Festivals, rang to ask whether he would be interested in coming to Glyndebourne and Edinburgh as production assistant to Carl. It was 1947. The opera was Glyndebourne's first post-war production.

Chapter 9

*Glyndebourne. Orfeo. Kathleen Ferrier. Rehearsal
problems. Carl Ebert and John Christie. Falling in
love. My parents say 'no'. Peter gets a divorce.*

My first impressions of Glyndebourne were that it was
idyllic but at the same time it was fraught for us dancers
because we had a dreadful choreographer. They were
going to do *Orfeo* with Kathleen Ferrier, and *The Rape of
Lucretia* with Benjamin Britten's company. For some
reason there was a bit of bad feeling – I think
Britten wanted John Christie to pay their expenses.

We, the dancers, all went down to Glyndebourne and the
artistic director, Carl Ebert, came on the stage with Peter.
'Peter is a nice boy,' he told us, 'but he's married.' At that
time Glyndebourne management hadn't known many
opera directors, and Carl said he'd like to have his son as
his assistant. So I thought, 'OK, don't touch', though I
knew he had already separated from his wife, Kitty, and
had two children.

Orfeo has these four big scenes: the introduction with
Eurydice, the *Hades* scene, *The Dance of the Furies* when
Orfeo goes down looking for her – that was the big dance
number – and then *The Elysian Fields*. Carl went right
through this, bar by bar, with Rupert Doone, the
choreographer, who didn't take anything in though Carl
wasn't to know that. To save us travelling up and down to
Glyndebourne every day, we rehearsed at Morley College
in London. We had learnt to dance the *Hades* scene, and
another dance for the *Elysian Fields*. Then came the day
when we had to go down to Glyndebourne and show the
dances to the Eberts. They couldn't believe it. They were
so dreadful. I don't know why they chose this

choreographer but I suppose there was probably a dearth of them after the war.

It was a disaster. We all hated doing the dances because we realised how ghastly they were. I think there must have been a big scene back-stage. Carl didn't actually sack Rupert – he kept the formal dances for the scene before *Hades* and showed us the steps he wanted by movements. In the *Elysian Fields*, he wanted a solo dancer to do a little walk up to a rostrum, take two or three steps, turn around, raise her arms, be ecstatic, then come down again. It wasn't easy. Carl chose three girls, one of them me, and looked at us all. I had a blue head band and he said, in his very thick German accent, 'I think we take the one with the blue whale (veil).' Nobody laughed, but that was me. It was a very fraught atmosphere, as you can imagine.

Kathleen Ferrier was marvellous. A lovely lady. At that time she had rather concentrated on doing folk songs and not much in the way of *Lieder* like most solo singers. But when we opened with *Orfeo and Eurydice*, she sang Orfeo and really carried the show. We had fantastic notices and the whole thing got by. I also had to do a little miming bit for Eurydice who sang off stage.

Peter always had to look after the ballet rehearsals but he never talked to me. He was a terribly shy boy. I was attracted to him but had written him off because he was married. We did have one funny episode.

The organ room at Glyndebourne is a lovely, long room with a bow window. At the time, there was a coffee counter at one end and couches down each side, fairly far apart. The artists used to sit there and watch the audiences strolling on the lawn. Then, blow me, one day I go in to have a coffee and Peter's there having one too. No one else. So I sit down on the other side of the room, you can't believe it nowadays that I was like that. There was a

43

phrase in the war 'How's your life?' If you met an airman, it was lucky he had a life at all. It was one of these catch phrases. So I said, to break the ice, 'How's your life?' And Peter said, 'She's in Switzerland at the moment.' End of conversation, it was so embarrassing.

I remember one day when they were rehearsing *Macbeth*, Carl said he wanted all the chorus to be absolutely still, just spitting out the words. He was very intense at rehearsals, nobody dared move or say anything without him. Fritz Busch thought that somebody wasn't singing. So Carl shouted at him: 'Work' (German accent). They both had a German accent. This happened two or three times. 'You,' he shouted pointing at one of the chorus. So this poor guy thought he was being told to 'walk' and started walking.

The following year, Glyndebourne went to the Edinburgh Festival to do *Macbeth* and I went back to London. Peter wrote me a note asking if we could meet for a meal when he came down. I was madly excited but didn't know which restaurant to chose. The friend whom I shared a flat with said why didn't we go to a Greek one in Soho because that would cut across barriers? So we did. Poor Peter. The waiter filled his coffee cup so full, right to the top, and he was so nervous meeting me and his hand shaking so much, that he didn't dare pick it up. We both felt there was something more. It was a magic moment you always hope for but never have.

He was still married to Kitty but living with friends and that whole period was very difficult. When my mother heard about this and that Peter had two children, it was terrible for her. Peter and I were seeing each other every day – he had a job with the BBC German service. I took him down to High and Over but my mother just couldn't accept him. She thought I was breaking up a marriage but it was already broken. She had just been through a decision-making time with my sister, Stella and now she had me causing trouble.

My parents were absolutely inflexible about Peter. They said 'No. Finished.' We must not see each other for three years. I always hoped we might meet by chance as we were working quite near each other. I was in other revues: Laurier Lister's *Tuppence Coloured*, which Joyce Grenfell was also in, and *Oranges and Lemons.*

I remember when I was going to be in *Tuppence Coloured* that I went with a friend to sign our contract with HM Tennent, the theatrical producers. They didn't know dancers got paid hardly anything. We'd been earning something like £8 a week, and they said 'would £14 be alright?' and we said, 'Well, yes.'

Peter and I didn't meet for a long time. He had to get Kitty sorted out and he was having a difficult time. In the end, he did get a divorce.

Chapter 10

Boy friends. Tuppence Coloured. Tea at
Glyndebourne with John Christie. Carousel. Venice
with Peter. Love in a mountain hut.

I had lots of other followers (boyfriends) at the time but I
didn't sleep with anybody, it wasn't like that. Well-
brought up girls didn't sleep with boy friends in those
days. I just had lots of offers! There was a professor of
engineering who was a friend of Bernard's, called
Geoffrey Hill, and he had two sons. They were all three in
love with me. Geoffrey once brought me an incredibly
expensive black dress from Paris and I accepted it – not
sure if he was expecting something in return. Whenever he
was in London he would take me out for a meal. Nothing
happened but he evidently thought he was my boyfriend.
Then his younger son, Desmond, when he was on leave
from the RAF, took me out. He bought a house off
Kensington High Street, did it up and took me to see it.
'This is where we're going to live,' he said. We'd only
been out two or three times, and it wasn't like that at all.

The other brother, Terence, a pig farmer, went to my
parents and asked for my hand in marriage before he'd
asked me. It then emerged that the two brothers hadn't
even talked to each other. How inhibited can you get? I
had another boy friend, Dennis, who was in *Tuppence
Coloured* with me. He had to sing a love song – I had a
lovely ball gown with a feather in my hair and we came
running on together. He was determined he would marry
me but I was already in love with Peter. Dennis told my
mother, 'Send her to Australia'. Nothing happened.

I was also going out with Baron, a fashionable society
photographer at the time, a friend of John Christie and also

of Prince Philip's, when Christie offered me his box at Glyndebourne, and invited me to bring a boy friend. Baron behaved very badly. He arrived late and you're not allowed in after the opera has started. That would have been a bad thing but then he photographed all those ladies in their clothes dragged out of mothballs after the war. I think the pictures were published in *The Tatler*.

Another time John Christie invited me to tea – I think it was because I knew his friend Geoffrey Hill. I remember it was in the parlour with the butler serving honey sandwiches. Christie was an amazing character, a real eccentric but always very friendly to me. He had his suits made by a tailor in the Cliffe area in Lewes and they were terribly baggy – he was so big, he just had to have something to cover him. Once he had a new dinner jacket made and it wasn't comfortable, so he took a pair of scissors and cut away behind the shoulder. Audrey, apparently, told him off and he said it was just more comfortable. Before they were married, Audrey, a lovely lady, was in the Carla Rosa opera company and Christie followed her around for several years before she said 'yes'. He was an opera lover, mostly Wagner, but Carl persuaded him Wagner wasn't suitable for Glyndebourne. 'You'd have to have the singers where the audience are, to make it big enough,' he said. He and Carl were both such strong characters. Sometimes Carl used to lose his temper if people weren't concentrating during rehearsals and start stamping up and down the stage; Christie loved it. He would sit and watch the rehearsals and go out and fetch anyone who was in the garden 'Come and see, Charles (Carl) has lost his temper.'

I was in *Carousel* when it first opened in London in 1950. Agnes de Mille was the choreographer and I loved her work. It was much freer and you could express yourself more. Classical ballet is very inhibiting – I hadn't realised how important expressing myself would be for me. When the Americans were auditioning for *Carousel*, it was the style of dancing none of us had ever done. We had to do 'double' work with dancing partners we'd never met. Normally you worked together for ages to get to know each other. At one point we had to be a family of nine, and they wanted to have a slope of dancers going down in height. Some of the girls had to go back for an audition four or five times; luckily, I came near the end, and got in.

It was when I was in *Carousel* and still not able to see Peter, though I always thought we might bump into each other accidentally, that he asked if I could take two weeks off to join him in Venice where he was going to direct *Cosi fan tutti*. I think it might have been the Glyndebourne production and with the cast mostly the same.

You don't usually take a holiday from a long running musical but we did have what they called a swing girl who covered for everyone. She was Maureen Swanson, who was a classical ballet dancer working in musicals and films. Afterwards she married the Duke of Rutland and became a duchess. At that time she was a very pretty little dancer and spent a lot of her time in the leading man's dressing room! He was an American guy, here for six months and then the part would be taken over by an English actor. This was the law at that time. When a show came from America, Equity let the American cast stay for six months and then they had to go back so the English actors weren't put out of a job. It was quite a good idea.

I got my two weeks off and went out to Venice. We had a marvellous time. The singers were lovely, we knew them from Glyndebourne, and we'd all go out to this gorgeous little restaurant. It was such a lovely group. There was a Spanish guy, and the Italian baritone, Bruscantini and his wife at the time, the soprano, Sena Jurinac.

Peter had made friends with an actor in the German

service of the BBC who had a mountain hut near Garmisch in southern Germany. He'd offered it to Peter and me to go to after Venice. And we did. We took a little train up into the mountains – I suppose we must have known we were going to do this because we had snow boots and clothes with us. We left our main luggage down in Garmisch with the agent, picked up the key to the hut and got into our boots. We were trudging up the mountain in deep snow with our rucksacks when a telegraph boy came chasing up after us to give us a telegram: 'Mother knows all. Return immediately'. So dramatic. It turned out that the actor who owned the hut was married to my cousin Deirdre and someone must have told my mother. It was bad news. We were rather short of money and had to pay for this telegram, but we didn't take any notice and just went on. Then another one came. We went on regardless and finally got to the hut. Inside, it wasn't really inviting, but it was very romantic. We had five days there and I always remember the stars. In the dark of the mountains, the sky was so clear. I couldn't believe how many there were.

Chapter 11

1951. Pregnant. Peter leaves his BBC job. We rent a flat for £1 a week. Wedding at Greenwich Registry Office. Tobias is born. Kitty and my stepchildren. Glyndebourne season.

I became pregnant before we were married. It was 1951, before the days of the pill and I was still in *Carousel* – I didn't stop dancing until after six months. Sally Gilmour, a star of the Ballet Rambert, had the main role. Peter had been living with friends for some time but I think me being pregnant helped him make up his mind about a divorce. He hated talking about problems, as a lot of people do, but I much prefer to talk about things.

It also triggered him into leaving the BBC. He had an interesting job producing for the German service, but he saw people who had been there all their lives. He was offered a permanent contract but felt he didn't want to stay there for ever. He gave in his notice but continued to freelance for them. It was a crazy thing to do really because he had no money and no capital and was leaving himself with a pregnant wife to be, and two little girls from his marriage to Kitty.

My mother at this point was very helpful. She got in touch with her brother who still owned a big Victorian house in Blackheath where she had lived as a child, that had been converted into flats after the war. One of them was vacant for £1 a week. Even then it was cheap. Peter and I were living in Earl's Court in one room, so that was a great help.

We were married in 1951 – someone wanted Tobias to be born legitimately – on a very foggy day at Greenwich

Registry Office at nine o'clock in the morning with Stella and my best friend Charlotte Mitchell, who had been in revues with me. She did sketches, rather like Joyce Grenfell. My parents didn't come and I don't remember minding. I knew they hadn't become reconciled to me marrying Peter. They gave us a silver teapot as a wedding present when, five years later, they came to visit us in Düsseldorf.

I wore a lovely, loose red coat to cover my enormous tummy, and afterwards we went back home to have breakfast. We didn't have a honeymoon, we'd had that in Venice. A difficulty with the flat was that it had no telephone and Peter had to walk to a phone box at the end of the road to see if the BBC had a job for him. We had one bedroom, a tiny hall, a little bathroom, a kitchen, living room and a conservatory at the back which you couldn't really use because it was so cold but which you had to go through to get to the loo. There was a garden and an old pear tree which my mother remembered from her childhood.

At that time, Kitty said she didn't want her children any more and would we have them? I said, yes, that was fine, so we all had to sleep in the one bedroom. Judith and Tabitha were about five and three and I got on well with them. Judith went to the King Alfred School, a modern boarding school in Hampstead which meant Peter had to take her from Blackheath, the other side of London, on a Sunday evening and bring her back on Friday. Later she went to Summerhill. I must say that both these schools were a disaster for her. I was open-minded about modern education and the only experience I've had of them was through these schools. They didn't give the children the stability they needed, for one thing. At that time, Summerhill was nearly all children from broken marriages and that made a bad atmosphere. Judith didn't learn a thing. Children chose their own subjects and didn't go to a class if they didn't feel like it. She was very gifted artistically but when she came to live with us later in Germany, she had no basis of maths and didn't know how to write a thousand!

Tabby went to the local primary school and was very happy and later to Dartington, and then Kitty suddenly felt she had to have her children back. She said we had taken them away from her. This was a big drama. Peter was working at the time so I had to take Tabby to London. But Kitty didn't want to see me, and I had to find someone to take both children to her. It was very difficult.

Tobias was born on January 30, 1952, and I started going to ballet classes directly afterwards. I wanted to dance at Glyndebourne that season and had to get into practice. I used to take Tobias in a wicker basket on a bus from Shooters Hill to Blackheath Station, a train to Charing Cross and then get up to Piccadilly. The ballet classes were in a studio above Augener's music shop near Liberty's in Regent Street. It was a big effort to get to the classes but I felt I had to otherwise I wouldn't have been ready for Glyndebourne that year and we needed the money

I did go back that year and danced in *La Cenerentola*, *Idomeneo* and *Macbeth*. Janet Moores, who looked after accommodation at Glyndebourne until she was tragically killed in a car accident near where she lived, had found us a cottage in Ringmer. She was told that the woman who owned it would look after Tobias but there was a bit of a misunderstanding though I didn't realise it, and I took him with me every day to rehearsals.

At Glyndebourne: Silvia, Peter, Tobias & Carl Ebert

At that time, the dressing rooms were around a courtyard. The pianist who had come to play for the ballet lent me a pram and a cot – she was a very kind woman. I'd get changed, put Tobias in the pram in the courtyard and the girl doing the props kept an eye on him. He just lay there and slept until I came back. He was a very peaceful baby. Peter was working flat out as assistant to his father.

Chapter 12

Glyndebourne at the Edinburgh Festival. Charles is born. Buy a house in Blackheath. Dance in Ciro's night club with Audrey Hepburn and at the Café Royal, Piccadilly. Peter on BBC course.

For the next few years, Glyndebourne was very involved in the Edinburgh Festival. In fact, they had been co-founders. In 1950 Audrey Christie and Rudolf Bing, Glyndebourne's general manager, had been walking round Edinburgh and Audrey said 'Wouldn't this be a lovely place for a Festival?' And Glyndebourne did become the central feature of the Edinburgh Festival, though they never had a proper opera house – they were in The King's Theatre.

Soon after *La Cenerentola,* I became pregnant again and Charles was born fourteen months after Tobias when we were still living in Blackheath. We decided we'd like to buy a house and went to an estate agent. He said he'd got one right on the Heath, and we should go and look at it. It was a very sweet Regency house by the pond with two rounded front walls, right next to the Greenwich Observatory. My parents had given us a down payment and we got a huge mortgage. The house was much too small and unrealistic for a family, but we loved it. We sent a surveyor in and he rang me up and said 'I can't see anything wrong with the house but there must be something about it because people never stay long. They always move on after a few months'. He said it was haunted and that Dick Turpin was meant to have slept there, that there must be 'some funny atmosphere'. I said, 'Oh well, we'll stay,' and we bought it. We painted the outside white, and I did all the little blue window frames. But blow me, we hadn't been there very long when Peter was offered a job in Hanover.

I was still in *Carousel* and after the performance I'd go down to Piccadilly to dance in the cabaret at Ciro's, a fashionable nightclub near Leicester Square. It didn't come on until very late, about 11.30pm to midnight, and part of our contract was to have an evening meal after the show. They also had Paris fashion houses putting on shows so the evenings finished later and later, not until about three in the morning and there weren't any trains running through to Blackheath at that time. I could go as far as Lewisham, but then had to walk across Blackheath. I didn't mind because I was used to walking alone in the night from when I was in Amersham, but once the police picked me up and said, 'What are you doing here?' and I said I was walking home and explained. And they said, 'While we're on duty, we'll take you home. It's not allowed but safer for you'.

Audrey Hepburn was dancing in the cabaret – she'd been in *Sauce Tartare* and the impresario, Cecil Landau, had spotted her. When she left the cabaret to make her first film, I took over the compering from her. We had a lovely Jewish comedian called Miriam Karlin who was very strict about her religion. When it was a Feast day, she didn't come in, which meant we couldn't do our quick changes. I did a *Lederhosen* dance and there was a tenor, Marcel LeBon, who sang a couple of songs. Just a floor show really. Later, we went on and performed in the Café Royal in Piccadilly Circus.

I think dancers felt Audrey Hepburn wasn't a very good dancer and actors that she wasn't a very good actress, but she looked amazing. When she was making the film *The Secret People*, she had a solo part and we were all in it, too. That was before she made *Roman Holiday* with Gregory Peck. We always looked on her as the leader because of her aristocratic background; her mother was a baroness. They had both escaped from Holland during the war and Audrey was supporting her mother on her miserable dancer's salary. She was very sweet, very shy, very quiet and unassuming, and very hard up. Cecil Landau got her to have the lovely gamin hair cut that really made her at the time. I remember Marcel LeBon invited her to go to a first night with him. She told us she had nothing to wear and no money, so she made herself a dress. She took incredible trouble with how she looked. She came in the next day in floods of tears because Marcel LeBon hadn't said a thing. She probably looked amazing and he hadn't once said 'you look lovely'. She really minded.

Charles was born in 1953. He was a very big baby and was pressing on the diaphragm so much that it kinked the oesophagus and I was very sick. The little girls had to go back to Kitty. I had to sleep sitting up in bed so that the baby didn't push up too much. It was March, freezing cold, and there was Peter all snuggled down under the bed clothes. I remember having labour pains and saying to Peter, 'it's fine, we'll take a bus to hospital'. But it was evening and buses were few and far between. Peter began to get very nervous. We got one in the end but Charles wasn't born until morning when I had a perfectly natural birth and out came this big beautiful baby. Stella, my darling sister, had two *au pair* girls for some reason and she lent me one.

Peter got a job on a new BBC course to train people to be TV directors, designers, everything needed for television. He got paid while he was on it and given a TV set; not many people had one at that time. He chose a producing course and later, when Glyndebourne performances were being broadcast on BBC TV, he always worked with the producer. We had no money but Peter met interesting people. Peter Rice, the designer, was one of them and they became lifelong friends.

I was a stay-at-home Mum that winter, looking after the two babies and the little girls who were coming and going between Kitty and us, which was difficult and upsetting for them and for me. I did meet her once before we were married. I think we had lunch and she tried to persuade me it was all no use. She wanted Peter to be with her but didn't want him to have a job. She was very artistically talented and kind of bohemian. She didn't really believe in marriage but Peter was her third husband. She never made another relationship and never took up a career. We helped to support her until the end of her life and she lived to be 97.

After Charles was born, I had to get into practice for Glyndebourne again. Peter was on the BBC course commuting from Blackheath in to London, but he always managed to get the Glyndebourne period free so he could assist his father, whose English wasn't that fluent at the time.

Chapter 13

Accommodation problems. Family dining at
Glyndebourne. Moran Caplat. Peter is offered job in
Hanover. Life in Germany

That year, 1953, we bought an old taxi for £23 and drove
down to Glyndebourne in it. It didn't have a petrol gauge
and, of course, we ran out of petrol – it was lacking a lot of
things, really. We all had to sit and wait for Peter to walk
to the next village to get petrol and there we were – the
German girl who was helping me with the children, the
two step children, Tobias and the baby, Charles, all
waiting for Peter to get back.

Our old taxi

We rented a house in Barcombe but soon things started to
go wrong. The German girl helping us got scarlet fever –
total panic. Judith and Tabby had to go back to Kitty again
and I don't know how I managed to cope. It was very soon
after Charles was born and I was thin as a rake. There are

pictures of me at that time and there is hardly anything of me. I think it was the dancing and all the worry. Then the people in the cottage said they didn't want us there and chucked us out. I still don't know why. Perhaps the babies were too noisy.

We moved to a flat above a dairy in Fisher Street in Lewes and lived there for the rest of the season. It was OK but rather difficult. I remember the milkman arriving very early and waking us up. But it was lovely dancing with the same choreographer, Pauline Grant, though her husband was gambling away all her money. She used to commute to London and when she got to Victoria Station, he would be there waiting for her to hand over her wages.

Fritz Busch had died in 1951 and Vittorio Gui was conducting. He was very keen on Rossini operas and we did a lot of them. Because I was married to Peter, we always had our meals in the canteen at a family table – Peter and Carl, and Gertie, Carl's second wife, and me. It was lovely. We used to discuss how dreadful the food was – I felt so ashamed to be English with these foreign singers having to eat it. When the season started it was drumsticks for us because the restaurant had chicken breasts. In the canteen, we had cold drumsticks, drumsticks stewed, drumsticks curried. Moran Caplat, who was general administrator for 30 years, always had a special meal for himself. I felt quite angry about this and later, when I was more mature, I wrote to him and complained. Moran Caplat replied saying it was 'very good English food' and I said, 'Well, you hadn't tried it.' I think he didn't get on too well with the Eberts. In his book, *Dinghies to Divas,* he told one or two rather unkind stories about Carl, which was a shame.

About a year later Peter was offered a permanent year-round job in Hanover as director of productions at the Stadtoper Hannover. (*Hannover is spelt with two 'n's' in*

Germany). It was heartbreaking in a way because we'd been in Blackheath such a short time. Peter went out to do a production to see how he got on, it went well and they offered him a contract to work there. So we let the Blackheath house and moved to Hanover where the theatre found us a flat. We were there for six years and Peter really learnt the whole opera repertoire there. He did something like eight productions a year, which was a lot. And we had the summers in England at Glyndebourne.

Hanover had been terribly bombed in the war, but we had a post-war flat right in the middle of the city though, when I look back, it was still very old-fashioned. There was a boiler in the kitchen and I had to fetch the coke for it from the cellar, no lift. Peter would get a hod full before he went to work and if I had to fetch some during the day, I had to take the two babies with me. Tobias was very late walking so we had to go up and down these stairs – we were on the third floor. And there was no hot water in the kitchen. In the end we had to put in a kind of Ascot heater ourselves.

I didn't speak German and Peter used to go off to the theatre every day. I once found myself in a butcher's in the street where we lived and one of the customers, realising I didn't understand the language, let me know that it was actually a horse butcher. Everyone was also very nice to me in the theatre where Peter was working. It was near our flat and I used to go to performances and after-show parties.

Silvia in the brothel scene, The Rake's Progress, Edinburgh festival 1953

When we came back to Glyndebourne that year (1953) I was dancing in *Alceste*, *La Cenerentola* there, and *The Rake's Progress*, *Idomeneo* and *La Cenerentola* in Edinburgh. It was on our trip to Edinburgh that our old taxi died on us. I thought we would leave the babies (Tobias and Charles) in Sussex with my mother and the German girl but found I just couldn't manage without them. So my mother put the girl and the babies on a sleeper and Peter and I drove across from Edinburgh to

Glasgow to pick them up. On the way back to Edinburgh bits of the engine just fell off. We were stranded miles from anywhere and Peter had a rehearsal. We must have got back somehow.

Chapter 14

Burglary at High and Over. The house is sold. Paul is born. Michael Redgrave and Equity wages. Jessica is born. Andrea is born two years later.

I can't remember exactly when my parents decided to leave High and Over. I think their marriage went through a difficult time after the war. Bernard had come home after years away and my mother had had a real slog during that time – she'd cooked for all those people for years and organised everything on her own. She was shattered and, I think, lonely. I remember her once saying she sometimes felt like a stranger in her own house because there was no one she wanted to talk to. And then Bernard came home and got a job at Fighter Command in Stanmore.

All the time he was away, and if he had any money to spare, he had invested it in rugs and beautiful carpets. He had been doing it for years – when he was in Iraq and later in India. When he was coming back to England, he had them carefully wrapped and packed up, but you never knew if anything was going to arrive because so many ships were sunk. In fact, nothing did for ages, and then they came. He had the most beautiful deep pile rug for their bedroom and I suppose there were about a dozen smaller ones in various sizes.

My mother had had a chap in to mend the stair carpet and not long after that, when she was staying in London, some people came at night with a lorry, rolled up all the carpets and rugs and drove off with them. All those beautiful rugs. Terrible. And my parents hadn't insured them. I think the police gave chase but ran out of petrol. It must have been awful for my father. I'm sure that stair carpet man had given them a tip- off. George, the gardener, sleeping on the top floor, hadn't heard a thing.

I think it was at that time that my mother said she didn't want to live at High and Over any more. 'I can't do it,' she said. Someone once asked Bernard what he'd do if he had to sell the house, and he said it would kill him. It was his baby. When my mother was really old, she told me she had never really liked it there. I said, 'What?' I had no idea. She said it was because it had always put them in debt to her brothers – all her family money had been left to them and she had evidently borrowed from them to finance High and Over. Bernard had contributed as well, but most of it was her money. And she hated being in debt.

Leaving High and Over was awful for Bernard. He was a very special man with a lovely sense of humour and, unusually in a scholar, very creative. They moved to a flat in Craven Road in London, the north side of Hyde Park, with a very big balcony and beautiful views. It was always full of plants – they both loved flowers. George and May stayed in the cottage at High and Over and brought them vegetables every week from the garden.

High and Over is still there and occupied but it's had a lot of ups and downs since my parents left. At one time it was divided into two but it wasn't suited to that. An Italian man and his wife put an incredible amount of money into it to try and get it back to how it was, but the land with the rose garden had been sold off for council houses. I think the house is now sometimes rented out for TV shows. It was when they were making such a fuss about me wanting to marry Peter, and my relationship with them was very bad. We didn't have much contact, so I didn't really know how difficult it all was.

My first glass of wine in Rome

In the summer of 1954 I danced at Glyndebourne in *Arlecchino*, *The Rake's Progress*, *Don Giovanni* and *Alceste,* and *Le Comte Ory* in the Edinburgh Festival. But I couldn't dance the following year because I was pregnant with Paul, my third baby. I became ballet mistress

Chapter 15

*Paul is born (1955). Paul Sacher. I play Fairy Queen
in Cinderella with Julie Andrews and Max Bygraves.
Michael Redgrave and Equity wages. The German
doctor. Jessica is born (1958), Andrea in 1960*

We were living in Germany and I was pregnant with Paul
but I wanted him to be born in England so checked in at a
London hospital. Paul Sacher, a Swiss conductor of
modern music and a close friend of the family, was
conducting *The Rake's Progress* at Glyndebourne and he
said to me, 'When this baby comes, if it's a boy, I'd like to
be his godfather.' And he was. It's why we called the baby
Paul, and Pauline Grant was his godmother. The
christening was in Ringmer, and my parents were there:
they'd come round to my marriage by then. We had a
lovely meal at the White Hart in Lewes and had put my
mother next to Carl; she was totally charmed by him.

Paul Sacher's wife, Maia, was a millionairess and heiress
to the pharmaceutical company Hoffman La Roche.
Hoffman, who was rolling in money, was her first
husband, Paul, her second, and she enabled Paul to buy an
orchestra. She was an incredibly talented art collector –
her dining room was peppered with Chagalls. But sadly
she got Alzheimer's disease fairly young though they did
everything to try and put it off. We were once planning to
visit them on our way through Switzerland, but Paul said,
'Don't come. She won't recognise you'.

Paul was quite a guy for the girls and after Maia died, and
he was in his 80s, he had another child and adored this
boy.

I was working a lot with Pauline Grant and she got me the

part of the Fairy Queen in *Cinderella* at the London Palladium. In the week leading up to it there was to be an autumn show – two performances a day, and three on Wednesdays. I'd always been a bit of an Equity girl. I'd started when I was on tour, speaking up for the dancers because the management never wanted to pay us until we'd done our Saturday show. They thought we might buzz off, I suppose, but we had to pay our digs on a Friday. The actor, Michael Redgrave, who was strong on Equity, asked me to call the dancers out on strike from this autumn show. It was the beginning of television and they were negotiating the first contract for dancers. We, the dancers, did come out and the show wasn't televised. The principal stars – I think George Formby was in it – were furious because they thought they were going to get nationwide coverage.

Cinderella must have been a lovely pantomime: Julie Andrews was Cinderella, Max Bygraves, Buttons. We had real little white Shetland ponies pulling the coach and I had to make the Fairy Queen's speech: 'But you shall go to the ball.' If the ponies made a poo in the middle, everyone laughed. They said I was the best Fairy Queen they'd had – I think quite often they had an actor for the part, not a dancer.

Later, Julie Andrews played Eliza in *My Fair Lady* in London with enormous success for years. So when it came to the film, she thought she'd get the role. She did all the Cockney scenes better than Audrey and when Audrey got it, she was absolutely devastated. Awful, really. Then Julie made *The Sound of Music* and had incredible success in that.

Three years after Paul, came Jessica (1958) who was born in Hanover. I didn't want to go to a German doctor so I didn't go to anyone. I think I may have seen one once and didn't like him. He just talked a lot and I found it difficult to understand him. And then he said, 'It's due on January 18. It must be called Wilhelm because he was the first German Emperor and his birthday was on that day.' That totally put me off. I said I wouldn't go back to him. It got nearer the time and I made an appointment with another doctor because I had to find somewhere to have the baby. I was booked in at a private nursing home and had an appointment for the next day but then she – Jessica, the first girl – came early, on January 10. I hadn't had check-ups or anything, but we did manage to get to the hospital in time. When I hear people talking about all these scans, check ups and blood tests, I think I was lucky – I had very straightforward births. The boys had to put up with a new sister. They called her the annoying sister. I hadn't given up dancing and used to go to classes for *Falstaff* – but there was always this enormous family packing up to do when we went back to Glyndebourne and Peter always managed to be working somewhere else at the time!

Two years later (1960), Andrea was born, also January 10, in the same clinic and on the same date as Jessica. Very convenient to have two little girls' birthday parties together.

Chapter 16

Peter is offered work in Düsseldorf (1960). Smallpox in the town. My stepdaughter Judith comes to stay. German schools. Polio. Return early for Glyndebourne season. Mark is born (1962). Peter finds a house, Ades, in Sussex, but no money to buy it. Stay in parents' house near Oxford. Jessica goes to school. We buy Ades.

Peter was offered a job in Düsseldorf and we moved there the following year. The director was keen on operetta but Peter wasn't. He liked ensemble opera where you have all your singers together, can rehearse them properly and they stay in the production. In Düsseldorf, it was organised more on the system of getting a singer in to sing a role. It wasn't his thing at all but he didn't realise it until he got there.

It was a town of head offices, much more elegant than Hanover. The theatre staff were meant to find us a flat but weren't able to – we now had five children. Finally, a friend of Peter's found one in Rheydt, a train stop from Mönchengladbach, between Düsseldorf and the Dutch border. Peter was working in Canada but as soon as he came back he had to go straight into the Düsseldorf job which meant that I had to move there on my own with all the kids. Of course, by the time the train arrived in Rheydt, the children were fast asleep and it only stopped there for two minutes – I hadn't even got their shoes on before it moved off. The guard told me he couldn't wait for us. I had to get off at Mönchengladbach and take a taxi to the flat. We were so short of money all the time – I still don't know how I coped, but we did.

I had all these little kids to look after but there were never any problems. They were lovely and there was always lots of laughter. Then, one day not long after we'd moved in, the theatre rang up and said they'd found us a bigger flat, did we want it? Peter hadn't started work in Düsseldorf yet and I had no idea what he was going to be earning and we didn't have a telephone. I'd have to ring him from the post office which was other end of town, to ask if we should take it. I couldn't leave the children on their own in the day, and had to go at night. I didn't have the money for the phone so raided all their money boxes and walked across town to make the call. Peter said, 'Yes, take it.' By this time we'd been in Rheydt three or four weeks and I'd got to know the flat and the little market. Tobias had settled in at school and had a lovely teacher. She had taken a lot of trouble with him, an English speaking child. But when Peter got back, we did move to the bigger flat. It was in Stadt Mitte, the middle of the town, and it was enormous, acres of it. I didn't like it much, it had no garden, but was very near the Rhine and there was a lovely, wide strip of grass running down beside it. I went out every day for a good walk with the children. Jessica was three and the queen of the playground. She was fixated on being there and would call out: *lielatz*, her version of *spielplatz* (playground).

The flat was on the ground floor and rather dark, but had lots of room for the children to run about and was within easy driving distance of the theatre. But Peter wasn't happy there. It was a big company with one theatre in Düsseldorf, another in Duisberg. The *Intendant* running it in Düsseldorf was an operetta man whereas, as I said, Peter liked serious opera and a permanent cast. It was fairly chaotic and then one day we went there and it was very quiet; we discovered they'd forgotten to order the orchestra, it was playing in Duisberg. Everyone was sent home. That kind of thing happened because the organisation was so complicated.

My eldest step-daughter, Judith, came to live with us and we got her a job painting scenery there. It was a very good training for her. Sometimes Peter's aunt would come and stay and if I wanted to go away, she would keep an eye on the German girl as well as the children. Sometimes the German girl would leave – the aunt wasn't very much fun. Peter had taught me to drive in England and we'd bought a car. It was a Triumph Herald, but wasn't really a family car. I think it was a two-seater but you didn't have seat belts in those days and six of us used to pile in and go to the English church.

We were in Düsseldorf for two years but Peter had always arranged his contract so that he was free to go to Glyndebourne each summer. The first year we were there (in Düsseldorf) someone arrived with smallpox; the whole town was put into quarantine and everyone had to go to the town hall to be vaccinated. Because Peter worked for the town, he had priority and we were sent there on the first day. We drove to the Town Hall and queued. We were told to strip down to our vests and wait on the stairs. But the German girl and I were not wearing a vest: we were both there in our bras which was quite embarrassing. My mother had had me vaccinated on my leg because she didn't want me to have an ugly scar on my arm and this added to my embarrassment when I had to show a leg for them to check it. They gave me another vaccination anyway.

Although I didn't like the flat very much, we did have good neighbours. It was very much an embassy area, and I made friends with a nice woman from the American embassy in Thailand who was living in Germany at the time, and another woman on the other side who one day rang our bell and said: 'I am unfortunately your neighbour.' I suppose she'd heard all the children having a ball in the morning, jumping around on their beds. But she was a lovely woman.

It was hard work. I was cooking for nine people all the time – lunch and an evening meal, German and English food. When the children were small, there were so many of us that I used to say, 'Wouldn't it be fun if we washed up?' I got a system going because on the whole you tend to ask the one who is most willing, which is not very fair. So when I didn't have help, they took it in turns. Each had a 'helping day' and the others could go off with a free conscience. It was nice for me to have quality time with one of them to help with the cooking and washing up.

Quite often I had to dress up and go to the theatre with Peter for first nights. Paul was at the English school which was for British Army children but very expensive for anyone not in the army – a lot of young teachers from Britain wanted to teach there. Tobias and Charles were at a German school, though that was a bit of a disaster. They had a shift system: one week the children would go in the morning and the next week in the afternoon, Catholic children, in the morning, Protestant in the afternoon, then they swapped over. By midday, the room for the afternoon class was stuffy and dirty. It wasn't a well-run school. Charles had only just started and was in a class with sixty children. Two classes had to be put together. I'd say, 'Charles, have you done your homework?' and he said, 'No one ever looks at it, why should I?' They have a much shorter school day in Germany than we do.

We were in our second year at Düsseldorf when Peter decided to leave. They had polio in the town and that was awful. One of the teachers in Jessica's *kindergarten* got it and died. When I went into a shop with the children, everyone was sort of hushed. The town couldn't decide whether it was better to close the schools and have all the children milling about the town or send them to school and infect each other. It was a very difficult time and I think we got so tense about it that the children and I went back early to Glyndebourne. In England at that time, there was an immunisation programme but because of our peripatetic life, I wasn't sure my programme was up to date. I remember getting a dose on a lump of sugar in Ringmer.

On the lawn at Glyndebourne. Left to right: Silvia, Paul, Andrea, Jessica and Peter

Family tree. Left to right: Jessica, Paul, Silvia and Andrea

I wasn't dancing in 1962 – I was pregnant with Mark – and after we left Düsseldorf for the final time, we rented a house in Seaford. We'd been in Barcombe but the owners wanted the house back and I couldn't find anywhere for the end of the season. Finally, the vicar at Barcombe said they had done up a house in Seaford and we could move there. The only problem was I didn't know where to check in to have the baby. Peter was sent a questionnaire from *Who's Who?* and he had to say 'none' to the question: what is your job, and 'none' to an address. My sister, Stella, said she would take my boys while I went into hospital in Brighton. She had three boys and a girl of her own and was going on holiday to Wales. She wasn't at all together domestically and it was very sweet of her to do it. I had the baby and stayed in hospital for ten days while Peter went house hunting

74

He came to see me and showed me a picture of a Georgian house in Chailey, a few miles from Lewes. I said, 'I think this is it'. So when I came out of hospital, we drove straight there. It was called Ades, and the owner, Mrs Peckitt, was converting it into three big houses. We walked in the lovely entrance and I said to Peter, 'do you mean you haven't made an offer?'

Ades, our house in Chailey

We immediately made one but didn't have any money to pay for it. At that time, Bernard had a guest professorship in Aberdeen and he said we could use their house for the autumn term. It was a lovely Victorian house in Iffley just outside Oxford, with a garden going down to the river. They had a punt and a canoe and they'd bought a house there for George, their old gardener, and May. At that point we thought Tobias and Charles should have some regular schooling and we sent them to board at Christchurch Cathedral School in Oxford. I had to buy uniforms for them and sew endless nametapes on football socks, tennis socks...... I designed a nametape which had Tobias Charles on the same one – Tobias' second name was Charles. They had a second-hand shop at the school where I could buy clothes and I made endless sweaters on a knitting machine.

We were still in my parents' house when they came back from Scotland. It was Christmas, I got pneumonia and they said we'd really have to leave. They just couldn't cope with us all. We had to organise a mortgage for Ades – we found a fantastic firm that gave us one and my aunt Hilda helped us out. Peter had a job by then and the people selling the house agreed to let us move in before completion. Tobias and Charles continued to board at Oxford and on Sundays they'd run along the towpath and have lunch with their grandparents. It was nice they could get to know them better. Paul went to the school later.

Jessica was four when we were in Iffley, very pretty, very shy and had been late learning to talk. We thought it might have been because our household was bilingual. We used to talk German to the German girl and English to Judith. Jessica had only just started to talk in German so when we got to Iffley in 1962, I thought it might help with her English and prepare her for going to an English school in our summer months at Glyndebourne, if she went to school there.

The headmistress of the primary school was sweet and I said, 'We have this little girl and she's very shy and only speaks German. Could you have her?' The headmistress said, 'I'm terribly sorry but I'm afraid we're full up.' And Jessica burst into tears, whereupon the headmistress fished out a hanky, gave it to her and said, 'OK, you can come.' Jessica was shy for a long time, but not now. Peter was shy, too.

The day we moved to Ades the snow was so deep our furniture couldn't be unloaded at Lewes railway station because the crane had frozen and couldn't lift the containers off the train. There was a big forecourt in front of the house and the water cock was somewhere underneath it. Peter was going all over the place trying to find it. It was a very big house. Each of the children had a room of their own on the top floor.

Chapter 17

I create a garden. Susanna is born (1964). Peter presents BBC TV 'Music in Camera' programme. He introduces Jacqueline du Pré to Daniel Barenboim. I run a ballet class in the village, teach deportment in a Finishing School. Prunella Stack. Peter goes to Canada for eighteen months. Difficult time for our marriage. Peter is offered work in Augsburg.

It was at Ades that I created my first garden. We had the middle section of the manor house and the garden area was just grass, more like a field than a lawn, and for our first few months, covered in snow. When we were able to mow it, it was remarkable how quickly it returned to a lawn. Having all these growing boys and girls, I decided the garden was mostly going to be used for football and other sports. We made a terrace on the south side of the house with a pergola to create shade for eating out and I planted vines and a rose to climb over it. Bernard bought fruit trees and planned our apple orchard. He was very knowledgeable about varieties and gave us a great selection and helped us plant them. When we returned to the house in 1980 we had a pool made, which was a great joy.

Our boundary on the left was a white-painted fence and I planted a hedge of red *Frensham* roses in front of it. In the flower beds by the house I planted lots of bulbs, lavender, herbs and many different tea roses. The soil was unrelenting clay and the roses loved it, but it was hard to work. In the 80s we bought more land and were able to have a vegetable garden including an asparagus bed. Peter had spent all his childhood living in towns, so wasn't knowledgeable about gardening, but there were lots of unskilled jobs to be done and when we lived in Italy in our old age, we both used to water the garden every evening for an hour.

I was dancing in *Macbeth* at Glyndebourne in 1964 until Susanna was born. She was a very small baby and I remember coming back from hospital and bending down with her to show Mark who was two, and him saying, 'Tiny baby, tiny baby'.

Peter was presenting a BBC TV programme called *Music in Camera*. The programme had been thought up by Humphrey Burton, then head of music, who planned programmes and asked Peter if he would like to present this one. The idea was to put two artists who hadn't met before to work on something together. The first two were Jacqueline du Pré and Daniel Barenboim and it was, of course, their first meeting. I don't really know if Peter liked interviewing. I'm not sure how well he got on with Humphrey Burton. But we had a regular salary, which was good with our big mortgage.

Living in Chailey, we got involved in village life. I started a ballet class so my girls could have lessons, and a friend played the piano. There were about a dozen children, mainly girls, perhaps one boy, and they asked me to do a production in someone's garden. Jessica was much the most talented child and so I gave her the main role, shared with another girl, and everyone thought the other girl should have had it! Mark was a bird in *Sleeping Beauty*. I enjoyed teaching the talented children, but otherwise it could be quite a slog.

I also got a job to teach deportment at a Finishing School at Cuckfield Park, a lovely country house, near Haywards Heath. I remember some of the girls were shy about their bust. They'd probably only just got one and they'd walk as if they were hiding it. You can tell peoples' characters the way they walk. The headmistress asked me to talk to the girls about birth control but I said I didn't think I was a very good advertisement for it.

When I left, I recommended Prunella Stack. She had done a lot for the Women's Health and Beauty movement. In fact I think it was called The Fitness League then. I didn't know her but she invited us to dinner when we were negotiating the job and I dropped the most awful brick. Before dinner we'd had sherry and when we sat down her husband came round with the sherry again. 'Would you like some sherry?' he asked. And I said: 'In my glass or in the soup? My mother often put sherry in boring soups.' In fact, it *was* a boring packet soup but I felt terrible about it. The children have never let me forget it. It was at this time I had my last year at Glyndebourne. I didn't feel too sad about it because Peter wasn't involved there any more.

It was while we were in Ades that Peter went to Canada for eighteen months. He got a job teaching opera at the University in Toronto and we decided we couldn't move all the kids over there.

Once, he arranged for me to go out and visit him but then changed his mind and asked me not to come. I guessed what was happening before I went, that he was having an affair with one of the singers. I said I was coming anyway. It was difficult. He was doing *Pélléas and Mélisande* and asked me to bring a wig for this girl, Daniele, that Glyndebourne was going to lend her. I felt resentful having to do this and in the end it was never used.

Then Peter got an offer to go to Augsburg, in southern Germany, as *Intendant,* the first time he would be theatre manager. It was a big step. He accepted the offer and after six years in Ades we decided to let the house, and go and live there. I thought this could be a new beginning for our marriage. At that time, he was also working twice a year for Scottish Opera and I was going up to one of his first nights. Getting up at 5am for an early flight, he told me that this girl had got a scholarship to study in Munich and he was going to give her some roles to sing when we were in Augsburg. That was bad.

I was desperate of course. It seemed like the end of the world. I had a good think about it. I thought, we've built up this lovely family and a lot of people's lives would be affected if we separated. I'd just have to put up with it. I asked Peter if we could have our marriage on a sort of open basis, if he would say when he was going to go to her. And he said, no, he couldn't do that. I had the burden of knowing about it and dealing with the children who didn't know. Well, I thought, someone has to be strong, don't they? I suppose in a way it was quite understandable. To be away for eighteen months, you can't expect a man to be celibate all the time. But it was a dangerous time for our marriage.

I recently told Jessica, Andrea and Mark about this period and they said they hadn't had a clue about it.

Chapter 18

English girl helping with the children says she's pregnant. I offer to adopt baby. A false pregnancy. Peter has work problems. Dominic is born (1968). Tobias and Charles at Lewes County Grammar School. Peter offered job as Intendant, in Bielefeld. He agrees to stay three years. Leaves after two when offered job in Wiesbaden.

Augsburg is in southern Germany, near Munich and had been heavily bombed during the war. It's an ancient town, very near the mountains and there was always snow from the middle of November to March. I liked it. I didn't have to do much driving, but had to put in quite a lot of appearances and lots of first nights and parties to go to, to support Peter. It was his first job as theatre director, the *Intendant.*

I was seven or eight months pregnant with Dominic and the day we arrived, the furniture hadn't come, something had gone wrong with the container. There we were in this empty house which was actually two flats that the owner was renting as a house. I had an English girl, Rita, from Chailey Secondary School, helping with the children. She was only 15 and very sweet, but I said to her before leaving Chailey, 'Rita, you don't speak any German, and you'll be lonely.' And she said, 'No, I absolutely want to come with you.' Because she was so keen she used to come after school before we left, to get to know the children.

She was one of triplets with an identical twin sister (who was pregnant in England at the time) and a brother. I was worried about what she was going to do on her day off but she seemed happy going out with American soldiers stationed there. Then she told me she was pregnant. I reckon one of them probably kissed her and she immediately thought she was. I'm not sure she had ever been told the facts of life. I said, 'Never mind, Rita, I'll adopt the baby,' but I thought, my God, it wasn't my fault. I hadn't wanted her to come with us. We got the local doctor to come and examine her in our flat so she didn't have to go to his surgery – she didn't speak any German – and he confirmed she was pregnant. The next time he came, she was bleeding, and he said 'she'll lose the baby,' but she hadn't been pregnant at all. She went back to England and they established it was a phantom pregnancy. We gave her a good reference!

When we first arrived, there was a minister for culture in the town council, a lovely man, but he retired and a younger man took over, a primary school teacher and incredibly jealous of Peter. It wasn't a good partnership. I remember they auditioned a Hungarian conductor who'd been given powers that were in Peter's contract, such as casting. He was quite nice and quite funny. He once said to Peter, 'You know Hungarians go into a revolving door after you and come out first.' He managed to get Peter out.

It was a difficult time, too, because the chap who owned the house we were renting, an awful man who often got drunk, didn't like us. I don't think he quite realised we had so many children and we probably didn't keep the flat as he wanted it. While we were there he started converting the top floor into a flat for himself and his girlfriend, and they would come up our staircase. I was a nervous wreck by the end.

What with one thing and another it wasn't a happy time, but it was very busy. Peter's job was very demanding, he was very much a public figure and didn't see a lot of the children. When he had an evening at home, it was a big event. I was talking to Mark about Peter the other day and he said, 'Well, Daddy was never there.' It was really a bit like that.

Tobias and Charles had stayed behind in England to finish their schooling at Lewes County Grammar School. Tobias was doing his A Levels and Charles was a year younger. The woman who had played the piano for my ballet class had a friend who lived by the railway halt between Seaford and Newhaven. She had three boys and a girl and I was told she might be able to put my boys up; she'd be grateful for the money, and the boys could take the train into Lewes each day.

Paul went to a monastery school in Augsburg and, poor boy, they'd done Latin intensively there every day for two years, and he hadn't done any. He had learnt German before so that came back, but Latin was difficult. They were very sweet there, they helped him a lot and didn't mark his homework. He was such an attractive child, everyone helped him.

A rather nice *répétiteur* we knew living in Bielefeld heard about Peter's difficult situation as *Intendant* and told him they were looking for one (an *Intendant)t* in Bielefeld, why didn't he apply? And that was what happened. After five years in Augsburg, Peter's contract was finished and he didn't want to work with the Hungarian any more.

Chapter 19

Bielefeld. Wiesbaden. Andrea and Jessica go to John Cranko's ballet school in Stuttgart. Problems at school for Susanna.

Packing up to leave Augsburg on my own with all those kids was a nightmare. Peter was working in South Africa – he sent me a postcard of an ostrich with eight little chicks following – it was meant to be me moving. I think Tobias and Charles came to help.

We drove to Bielefeld and Peter had found us a flat. It was a small provincial town with a climate very like England. (Paul married a Bielefeld girl who says she wants to stay there until they die!) There was a lovely music director and it was a happy time. Peter said he'd stay there for three years but after two he was offered a job in Wiesbaden. I was really angry with him. I was still feeling rather bruised from our marriage problems and knew moving to Wiesbaden was a mistake. But it was a more prestigious position for Peter, in a state theatre, rather than a town one. It meant another move for us and another change of schools for the children. Dominic started school there. He was about five.

Once Susanna didn't go school because she only had one scheduled lesson and you weren't allowed to take the children home after just one. That got a letter from me – I'm famous in the family for writing letters – I had to sort things out. I knew the minister for culture in Wiesbaden and he contacted the school and told them the wife of the *Intendant* had had to come to him to complain about the school. After that, Susanna was given a full programme of six lessons though the others didn't have so many. I don't think she minded. She was a very keen little girl. The theatre in Germany gets a lot of money, but the schools don't. I remember one year the school children went on a march – they needed more teachers, books and paper. What I thought scary was that some of the parents wouldn't let their children march in case they got put on some list: traces of the Nazi era, I suppose

We were three years in Wiesbaden, but it wasn't a happy time. Peter had an assistant who made out he was his friend, but wasn't. The same kind of experiences happened to Carl, Peter's father. I think people felt they had everything worth having and they wanted some of it too. There's a lot of jealousy in the theatre world. Wiesbaden was not a happy time for me either because of the town's politics. There were a lot of rich retired old people, and lots of posh flats. Opposite, on the other side of the river, was Mainz, a Labour Socialist town which I would much have preferred.

Jessica was due to move to high school and a friend of mine, Anne Woolliams, was going to be teaching ballet in Stuttgart under John Cranko, the dancer and choreographer and director of the Stuttgart Ballet Company. He'd joined the Royal Ballet when I did and I remember he always had trouble getting the *mazurka* step right. I took Andrea and Jessica over for an audition and Anne said, yes, she'd like to take them. She was starting a new boarding school and they could stay there. I used to have to drive them to Stuttgart every week, usually in the fog. When they weren't dancing, they had to go to a gymnasium, like an English grammar school, for lessons.

They loved it there, though they didn't like Anne. She was a very good but strict teacher, very demanding, all the girls were terrified of her. But she turned out some very good dancers who went on to the Stuttgart Ballet Company, which had a very high reputation. I was buying the idea blind really, but it seemed the right thing to do.
It was a big success and the girls had excellent ballet

tuition. Anne died rather young. She had endless hip transplants because the moment she had a new one, she went teaching again, and put her hip out.

Jessica got into a classical ballet company, but just like me, she found that quite stultifying. She began to meet people from a modern dance group and in the end she left the ballet company and joined that. Andrea started having trouble with her knees and in the end had to take time off. She came to live with us in Scotland then fell down the stairs and had a bad sprained ankle. Eventually, she had to give up the whole idea of being a dancer.

In Wiesbaden, they were gutting and renovating the old theatre and Peter loved the challenge of having to find different venues. The company had rented a cinema in the red light district where the opera performances would take place, but it was too small and audiences didn't like going there. But Peter made a success of it and other venues. He had a director of plays, Horst Siede, who was excellent, a lovely man, very far Left. Peter had wanted him in Augsburg but the local town council wouldn't have him because of his politics. He and Peter remained friends and when Peter went to Wiesbaden, he took him on. He did the most beautiful productions. It was a kind of collaborative group of actors. The only problem was that they all had their input so that everything took for ever. Someone committed suicide. Horst Siede had a way-out wife and the first time I met her, she ordered two or even three helpings of mussels which really surprised me. She was a pianist but never gave concerts.

Chapter 20

*Alexander Gibson, founder of Scottish Opera, invites
Peter to become administrator. We leave Wiesbaden
and move to Glasgow. Intrigue at the Opera House.
Staff trip to Lucerne. Financial difficulties at the
opera. Peter resigns. Return to Ades. Tenants won't
leave. We take them to court. Susanna and Dominic
go to Lewes Priory comprehensive school.*

When Alexander Gibson, the conductor, who had founded
Scottish Opera with Peter Hemmings in 1962, invited
Peter to become its administrator, we thought it was
manna from heaven, a perfect solution and we were not
sorry to leave Wiesbaden. Peter Hemmings, then the
Scottish Opera's administrator, had been invited to go to
Australia to run the Sydney Opera House but he didn't
have a happy time there and later wished he hadn't gone.
Of course, everyone wanted to succeed him in Scottish
Opera and everyone thought they were going to. But Alex
Gibson wanted Peter; he was very influential on the Board,
and Peter got the job. As he had been having quite a bad
time in Wiesbaden politically, it was great to be offered
this and we moved to Glasgow in 1977.

Peter was to do one or two productions a year but didn't
tell anyone except his employers he was leaving
Wiesbaden. No one else. One of my friends still holds it
against me that we didn't tell her we were leaving, but
Peter said, 'Darling, if you tell one person, it's going to get
out.' So we just left. I didn't understand why he minded
people knowing we were leaving.

He found us a lovely house in Glasgow. It had been owned
by some elderly people, one was handicapped, and they'd
installed a lift. It was in Kirkley Gardens, one of those

beautiful Georgian terraces. It was really cheap because the owners wanted to get rid of it. It was all painted green that I absolutely loathed and had great high rooms, a mauvey-coloured carpet, nine open fires, six loos and was near the botanic gardens. It was great.

We had three children at home: Mark, Susanna and Dominic. (Andrea and Jessica were in Stuttgart in the ballet school.) I couldn't face sending them to a Scottish primary school so they went to the High School of Glasgow which had a good reputation. Mark was just at O level age and Susanna was a bit younger but luckily both extremely bright. What I couldn't understand was how Mark could manage the Maths – in German you put the second digit before the first, like *vier und zwanzig*. How he went from that into the English system so quickly I just didn't understand. But he did fantastically well. The school called me one day to say how bright he was and I thought they were talking about Susanna because I knew she had a high IQ. No, no, the other one, they said.

Dominic, poor little soul, had to change schools again. He was only about five, and spoke only German – I think we mostly spoke it at home at that time. Andrea came over after she'd had her ankle injury and couldn't dance. She'd done a secretarial course, but didn't really know what she wanted to do. It was lovely for me to have her around and she helped me with the parties we put on for Scottish Opera. I had to do a lot of entertaining – sometimes a buffet for ninety people. I always seem to have been cooking for big numbers. We once had a Burns Night party and had to have haggis which I have to say I bought from a friendly butcher. It was a very social time and to start with it was lovely. I already knew Scotland quite well because Peter's mother lived in Haddington, just outside Edinburgh. Alex Gibson's wife was a friend of mine and so was Peter Hemmings' wife. David Pountney, who had been taught by Peter, was doing productions.

Peter wasn't a good judge of character and when Peter Hemmings left, he engaged a girl to be his assistant. She wanted Peter's job herself and did get it eventually, but it was a disaster and after six months she was out. Peter was traumatized by this. I don't think he ever really recovered. It was very stressful, especially as he didn't like talking about anything. He bottled it all up, it was just the way he was.

There was one occasion when the company had a guest trip to Lucerne, with two opera productions. The assistant came too. She'd been out to Lucerne and booked really posh hotels for about five of us, and really crummy ones for the stars. When we went there and I found what it was like, I said I couldn't stay in a smart hotel when others were staying in crummy ones. I said I was going to move in with the others. It just wasn't right, and Peter came too. At that time, someone from the company said to me, 'Peter is too trusting, he doesn't realise they are sawing away the legs of his throne.' It's what you say in German. And it wasn't very long after that Peter was intrigued out. In the end he resigned over a disagreement with the financial decisions being made.

We left Scotland and decided to go back to Ades. Mark had got into Glasgow University to read engineering and we'd found a flat for him. But the family we'd let Ades to didn't want to move out when the crunch came. They just wouldn't shift. We had an agent who was meant to be looking after the house for us but the family never paid what they owed. The father went off on trips. Sometimes he made a lot of money and would come back, go to The Five Bells, the local pub, and treat everyone to a drink. Their children went by taxi to the Rudolf Steiner school in Forest Row, about nine miles away – the same taxi every morning, and another two in the afternoon to fetch the children because they finished at different times. The wife ran up the most enormous taxi bills and when they finally did leave, they owed money everywhere. We had to take them to court and the judge said they should pay us £5 a week, but we never got it.

In the end we all had to stay in Glasgow with Mark – Susanna, Dominic, Peter and me, too many of us for that flat. But we worked on ideas for Ades and eventually, a year later, did get the family out. The house was in a terrible state: the kitchen had leaking pipes hanging off the wall; we really had to start restoring it from scratch to get it back into shape.

When we'd been in Chailey before, our three older boys were at the Lewes County Grammar school and the headmaster had been excellent. But when we came back in the 80s, it had become a Comprehensive. I took Susanna and Dominic to see it and to ask for an appointment with the headmaster. All three of us went into the teachers' room – some of them were from the old grammar school, so I knew them already. And they said, 'yes, of course, we can have the children, when would they like to start? Today? Tomorrow?' The children were looking at me and I said, 'Yes, today, that will be fine.' I don't think they've ever forgiven me, but I reckoned that to go home and worry about it and not know what was going to happen would be worse.

Chapter 21

We become founder members of the SDP. Peter elected Lib Dem parish and district councillor. Canvassing. Glyndebourne's controversial wind turbine. Susanna and I become bell ringers in Chailey church. I work in a health food shop.

It was at this time (1981) that we got interested in politics and became founder members of the SDP. I once had to arrange a public meeting in Lewes where the Liberals and Social Democrats were going on stage together for the first time. That was fine, but when I was welcoming people, one man said to me: 'Oh you must be somebody's wife.' I was speechless. How insulting! I nearly said I was a founder member of the SDP. Another time when we went to one of the SDP's conferences in Brighton, the organisers were very impressed with our membership cards because they said: No. 1 and No. 2. Funny how these things stay with you. We didn't really like the merger. As Liberals, I think we lost our identity, and it did become the Lib Dems in the end. I loved Shirley Williams, and *Testament of Youth* by her mother, Vera Brittain, was one of my favourite books.

We did a lot of local canvassing in Chailey and Peter became a Lib Dem parish and district councillor. He had always been interested in politics and would have liked to have read the subject at university, but his father couldn't have afforded it. He later realised that, as a German living in England, it probably wouldn't have been a good idea to go into politics anyway.

I quite enjoyed knocking on doors canvassing for Peter, though sometimes you could get so carried away, you'd stay too long. We had a difficult time when Glyndebourne wanted to install a wind turbine in their grounds and there was a lot of opposition from local people. No doors were slammed in our faces, though one person said he'd 'go up there and blow it up'. What annoyed me was that there is a row of enormous pylons stretching across the fields but people didn't seem to care about those. I think they are very unsightly and ugly and the wind turbine is rather attractive. I wrote several times to the local paper, the *Sussex Express*, I felt so strongly about it. Gus Christie, owner of Glyndebourne, got David Attenborough to come down to one of our big meetings. I think global warming is imminent and we should do everything possible we can to fight it.

We were active in Chailey church and friendly with the vicar, Eddie Matthias, who did a lot of good work in the parish, organising Beating the Bounds and other activities. Sadly, he got pancreatic cancer but still motivated people to do things. I think Susanna was the first family bell-ringer there – she was fifteen – and she asked me if I'd like to do it too. I did, but wasn't very good. We got Peter doing it as well, but he never had time to practise. It was fun, and they were a sweet group of people with whom I'm still friendly. I liked it because I felt I was doing something for the parish but think I always felt a bit inadequate. I also thought it would be good for my muscles! We did it for about seven years.

I've always been interested in healthy food and went to work in a health food shop in Lewes originally run by Patricia Bullard. Susanna came and worked there, too, after leaving school. I'd learnt a lot from my parents who had been very much into healthy eating – I always remember Bernard eating an enormous amount of nuts; my mother's family were from Switzerland where the health food movement started with *Bircher Muesli*. It was the 30s, their period. I hope I've passed my love of healthy food on to my children.

Chapter 22

I become Peter's assistant for New Sussex Opera's
Benvenuto Cellini. I assist him in Los Angeles. Peter
works with Carl, introducing children to opera.

It was in the 80s that I started working as Peter's assistant
which was great fun. He did *Benvenuto Cellini* for the
New Sussex Opera in the Brighton Dome, a very
complicated work with lots of chorus and dancing, and I
had to make sure everything ran smoothly. I had blank
pages between the music sheets where I wrote notes about
lighting and whatever Peter told the singers had to be
done. He couldn't read music, nor could his father – but I
could. He just knew what he wanted it to sound like.

Liaising with singers was lovely. I've been in the *genre* all
my life, dancing in operas, and I'd watched Carl working
and had worked with him too, so it was all in my blood.
Once in Los Angeles, a French opera team were trying to
get an opera company off the ground and Peter and his
father knew the director and his work. Peter Hemmings
was in charge of the company in its opening season and
invited Alex Gibson, the conductor, and Peter Hall to join
them. Both Peter Hall and Peter Hemmings were doing
expensive operas (*Macbeth* and *Othello*) and they needed a
third one to be done more cheaply. They asked Peter to do
Madame Butterfly, but he really shouldn't have accepted it
because the conditions were disgraceful. We thought it
would be fun with all the old team, but it wasn't. Our
Madame Butterfly was a very big woman, not a butterfly at
all! I went over and helped Peter – I was very meticulous
about learning the score and was very touched when Peter
said, 'Oh Silvia knows where we are.'

Carl, or Papsch, as I used to call him, was also doing

productions for children in LA with young professional singers, in an auditorium which seated 6000 people. There was a very enterprising character who ran a Music for Schools department with the idea of introducing eight-year-old children to opera. They came streaming in, in their yellow buses, the whole theatre was like a beehive. For several years, Peter went over to assist Papsch working on this; he introduced the opera and told the story and he had such a lovely personality, it was a big success. I think they did *The Magic Flute* and *La Cenerentola,* too. Some of the artists became famous singers and one of them dubbed the songs for Audrey Hepburn in *My Fair Lady*. They all adored Peter and we had a lovely time.

The first time we went to LA we stayed with friends of the Eberts who lived in Beverley Hills and I used to go for walks. I couldn't be in cars all the time. Once I was picked up by some policeman who said, 'What are you doing?' And I said, 'Going for a walk'. 'Crazy English lady,' they said.

I don't think Papsch minded Peter being in the theatre, because he'd come in by the back door as it were, and he loved having him as his assistant. It was worse for Peter because he felt people always thought he got on because of his father. But Christa, one of Carl's daughters and one of Peter's two step-sisters, a beautiful girl, married to Paul Cooper, a composer of modern American music and professor of music in Dallas, wanted to become a singer, but Carl wouldn't go and hear her sing or raise a finger to help her. He was terribly nervous of people not doing it well enough. Not being top class. He didn't mind me dancing and we had a very close relationship. We just clicked. It was lovely for me because of my parents being so distant, that I had this family instead.

Chapter 23

Peter's step-mother, Gertie, dies. Carl dies. Bernard dies at 94. My mother, 93, comes to live with us in Chailey. She and her sister, Hilda, go to an Exmouth care home. My sister, Stella, dies.

Peter's step-mother, Gertie, died before his father; Carl was well into his nineties when he became ill. His son, Mike, Peter's step-brother, lives in Los Angeles, Renata and Christa, his daughters, in Ann Arbor and New Jersey, both far from their father. They had been in Turkey when Papsch was working there during the war and always used to count in Turkish, even in their old age. Living so far away, they weren't able to help very much when Carl became ill and Peter and I used to go over from Scotland now and then to see him. We wanted to take him back with us and had converted part of our house for him. But his daughters got into a terrible state and said we were stealing their father from them. So he didn't come.

Bernard was 94 when he died and at the end he had skin cancer. He and my mother had been living in Peebles near my brother, Philip, in a lovely flat right by the River Tweed. I went up when Bernard was dying and stayed on afterwards with my mother. There was a memorial service for him in Oxford but when I wanted to go, I couldn't find anyone one in the family to come and look after my mother – she was too fragile to travel. So, I couldn't go. Funnily enough, I couldn't go to my sister, Stella's funeral either because Peter wouldn't let me go. He had become very dependent on me – I think I was his sort of security in the end.

My mother came to live with us for a while. She was 93 and I got on fine with her. We'd been through the war together when Bernard was away. But looking after an old person is very tiring. I felt I wanted to get out of the house and have a different kind of caring. She used to say, 'You're off to do your good works, are you?' when I was going to spend some time at Chailey Heritage, a hospital and school for handicapped children. I got very fond of some of the children and they were lovely people working there.

But there was suddenly a crisis in the family: I had to go to assist Peter in Germany, and Stella, who was meant to be taking our mother back to live with her in Scotland for a few months, just disappeared. She lived in Croydon by herself, and had been divorced for a long time. She had someone she called 'the man I cook for across the passage,' and I think she may have been worried about losing him if she went away. I didn't know where she was. I only discovered later that she'd gone to our cousin Gillian, and hadn't told me.

Stella's eldest son, Nick, was a chemist and had a friend who ran care homes in Exmouth. He suggested my mother went there – he knew they would be kind to her. She was very good about it. She said yes, of course, she could go. 'I don't want to be a burden'. We had another part of the family in Devon who visited her a lot. She was there for quite a long time and died after we moved to Italy.

Her sister, Hilda, a psychiatrist, went there too. She once told me, 'You very soon get as mad as your patients.' She opened a bookshop in Charmouth and I used to go down with the children on holiday and stay with her. She was a lovely woman. She always used to change for dinner, and when I went to see her she often had her best velvet dress on. She would talk to the news reader on television: 'George, I'm not feeling very well today'.

Stella died in a care home in Exmouth and her daughter

97

Judy lived nearby. She (Stella) had all kinds of things the matter with her and in the end her body wasn't making any red corpuscles. She would only live, she told us, if she had blood transfusions which took a whole day and which she found very tiresome. The last time I went down to see her, we discussed the whole business. She said she had to decide whether to live or die and didn't know what to do. She died that night and I was very glad she didn't have to make that decision. She donated her body to research.

Chapter 24

I help build a house in an organic vineyard. Peter retires. We go to live in Italy.

It was when we were living in Chailey, and I was in my sixties, that I helped build a house.

When Susanna left school she had a gap year before university. She became editor of a magazine called *Country Weekly* and ended up writing most of the articles, too. One day she saw an advertisement for people to go on a house-building course in an organic vineyard in Sedlescombe in East Sussex. It was for three weeks and you could get a family ticket. In that time you would build a house that had been specially designed for amateur builders and live in a tent on the site. Susanna said, 'Mum, why don't you do it?' So I said, 'Alright, I'll have a go'. I think we'd already thought we might go to live in Italy and that this skill might be useful. Pam, Tobias' wife, was keen to do it, so she and I went right through the three weeks. Because it was a family ticket, some of the family came over, just for a day.

It was a very funny mix of people. There was a dentist who had retired from a practice in Dubai and wanted to renovate a house in Scotland and be able to oversee the building. There was a very funny chap who came with his wife and they lived in a tepee and were a member of WWOOF – Working Weekends on Organic Farms as it was known then. It's now World Wide Opportunities on Organic Farms. I was put in charge of what they called a birdsmouth, a little triangle in the rafters that another rafter slotted into. They gave everyone a turn of being in charge but the man in the tepee said he wasn't going to work under a woman. It was a bit ridiculous really. The course was cooked up by two chaps: one of them gave lectures on electrics and another on sewerage so we had a talk about electrics in the morning and did the work in the afternoon. Then we learnt about sewerage.

We were building it for the couple who owned the vineyard. I wrote an article about it for Susie's magazine, and when I went back to have a look at the house with Peter, 18 years later, my article was still pinned up in the porch. It wasn't a very nice house, mostly wood, except for a brick chimney built in the middle by one of the chaps running the course. It was going to have two storeys and the only professional help we had was to have a crane driver erect the wood frame.

I didn't have a head for heights but when the rafters were there with their different layers, it was much better because there was a sheet of insulating material over them and you couldn't see the awful gap below.

It was OK when the weather was nice, but awful when it was raining. It was really dangerous all the way through. One day I was up on the roof, it was very slippery and pouring with rain and I remember saying to the young man organising the group, 'Paul, I really don't think this is my thing'. He said: 'Go on Silvia, you can do it.' So I did. When the rafters were up, you put battens going the other way and I was able to walk along them quite quickly, with my feet turned out, as in ballet, but with nothing to hold on to.

Silvia on the building site

Putting the roof on.

The couple who owned the vineyard had been living in a caravan and there was a kind of shed which was our only washing and eating place. The loo was so disgusting that Pam and I both used the woods. It was a very primitive arrangement and all rather chaotic. I don't think any one else washed – I used to go very early. Pam and I shared a tent and she was very frightened of insects so every night before she came into the tent, I had to vet it.

One evening, we thought we'd go to Bexhill swimming pool and have a shower. I rang the office and asked when they closed and they said, 'Well, you won't be able to use the pool after 6pm' – we didn't stop work until 6.30pm – 'but you can use the changing room and shower'. We had made friends with someone with a car who drove us over. We were really filthy with mud-encrusted boots, and looked awful. We went into the changing room and there were all these young girls in purple lycra outfits sitting there just having come from their keep-fit class, doing their nails. I never felt so dirty in my life. Once Peter came and took us home for the weekend. He joined us on the last couple of days of the course, and we did the sewers together. Quite an amazing thing to do, really

And we did build the house. I remember one morning the postman came and said 'Blimey, there wasn't a house here last week.'

The children thought it was very funny that they had a mother in her sixties doing this. Toby came over one day and didn't recognise me. I was in dungarees and probably a bit dirty. He said, 'Oh, Mum…' I was glad I did it – I think I'm less frightened of heights since then and I think my children were quite impressed. I thought it was quite an achievement myself, in a way.

Around this time Peter was thinking of retiring. He was in his seventies and work had rather tailed off. He thought he'd had enough. Years before I'd seen an advert in a paper about a couple who were buying derelict farmhouses in Italy and marketing them. I'd cut it out and kept the address. It was in Citta di Castello in Umbria. Why did we choose Italy? Well, I felt I had roots there. I'd lived in Rome with my parents until I was three years old and Peter had done several productions there and loved it. And we had our honeymoon in Venice. So we had a kind of connection. Once I did an interview with the German service of the BBC about whether we would live in Germany or England when Peter retired and I said, being diplomatic, well, maybe Italy.

Chapter 25

We fall in love with a derelict farmhouse in Umbria.
We sell Ades. We buy the farmhouse, restore it and
create a garden. Life with the neighbours. Builders.
Shopkeepers. Music festivals. We run a B&B.

We decided to get in touch with the company who'd advertised properties and went out to find a house. The agency seemed very well-organised and gave us lots of folders to look through. We did find a house but it was a ruin. The next day the girl in the office put us in her car and took us around. But we couldn't find anything we really liked.

The following day we had a picnic in Assisi. It is a beautiful area and we thought we'd have one more go. We went back to the agent and she said, 'Well, we do have another house. We haven't seen it ourselves yet, but we'll go there.' And that was it. We knew immediately we wanted it. We said, 'Yes, we'll have it.' We weren't daunted by the derelict state of the farmhouse, we were excited. The agent was flabbergasted we could decide so quickly, but the position was perfect. It stood on a hill and had marvellous views, pretty well 360 degrees. The land was planted with olive trees and sunflowers.

We sold Ades to a couple from South Africa who said it was just what they wanted. They were buying a house in London, a big house in Sussex and wanted something else. They were buying it through a firm who found properties on behalf of very wealthy clients and they were incredibly fussy – they took the staircase apart to see if there was woodworm. It was rather a nightmare but we did get a good price in the end.

We made an offer for the house in Italy. We didn't have any doubts, but the children did. 'What have Mum and Dad done now? They've bought a ruin'. It was on the market for £49,000 and being sold by farmers in the valley. Afterwards one of the sons dropped in for a coffee and said we hadn't paid enough for it. 'But at the time,' we told him, 'You were happy with it'.

We left England in 1990 and had fourteen lovely years in Italy. It was 'goodbye, England, hello, Italy and *Col di Mura*,' our new home in a little village called Monterchi.

The house wasn't ready for us to live in and we stayed with a New Zealand guy, Rob and his wife Jane – they were in a converted farmhouse down the hill. We'd met them having Italian lessons in Brighton when they'd bought their house and we were in the process of buying ours. Peter's Italian accent was very good because of opera, and he knew lots of words like *amore,* but not much use when you are buying a house. I had German and a bit of French, but we never got fluent in Italian and the people around us spoke with a broad dialect.

The company marketing the house had an agent called Fabio who organised the builders for us. He was a rogue, but a charming one. You never quite knew if he was above board or not and we were rather hampered with all his builders' love affairs. One couldn't come this week, he'd say, because his girl friend was having a baby. But the builders he recommended were good and we got them to put on a new roof and do the bathrooms. One day Fabio came and said, 'I have one nice thing for you and one not so nice. Which would you like?' And I said, 'Well, we'll have the not so nice one first, and that was the bill. The nice one was he'd brought us a kitten. We needed a cat, he said, with all these mice around. We took the cat and within about six weeks, she gave birth to five kittens. It was fun and I think Fabio was OK.

105

When we first moved we were very busy putting the house in order. It was big – I'd always wanted one that was open-plan, with light and space. I think my style was very much influenced by High and Over. There were three floors with a large bedroom at the back, kitchen in the front, and a big sitting-room that we cut in half to make a bathroom and Peter's study. A ladder with wide steps led up to the attic floor which had another two big bedrooms in the roof. It made a lovely nursery for the grandchildren. We called one of the rooms on the ground floor The Cow Stall because it had a built-in manger along the back wall like a trough, and you could see where the cows had rubbed their sides along it. It was like a sculpture of blackened wood.

Col di Mura, our house in Italy

After we'd restored the house, we worked on converting the tithe barn into a summer residence for us when the house was full. We built a terrace with a wonderful view over the countryside and spent a lot of time there. We had incorporated a small sleeping-out balcony, and lying there on a warm summer night with millions of stars, fireflies and the perfume from the roses, was idyllic.

Over the years I've made a few gardens from scratch but the Italian one was the biggest. I wanted to make it merge into the landscape, nothing too formal. Sometimes the adjoining fields were sown with sunflowers, which were spectacular.

The garden was really a field of a couple of acres, with 60 olive trees. We were able to harvest the olives and take them to the castle in the village where they had a press. We planted our favourite English apple trees, imported dozens of rose bushes which thrived in that terrible soil, not really clay, more like shale. The Italians are funny about flowers – I saw a lovely rose in someone's garden when driving through a village, so I got out and asked what kind it was. And he said: 'A rose'.

I really let the garden develop slowly. I planted clematis and vines on the pergola, cypress trees, a magnolia tree, and a pine for shade. We put in kiwi fruits which grew well but which I'm allergic to – my throat swells up – but which everyone else enjoyed. There was a walnut tree at the back of the house; local people told us they always had one outside loos because it kept flies away. We had a swimming pool built but we did all the tiling round it ourselves with family members to help, and I planted lavender down a steep bank leading to it. I made a fountain out of flower pots. There were several olive trees at pool level so I made low-containing walls round them and planted Alpine strawberries, which worked well. You could smell them when just over-ripe while you were swimming. We laid all the tiles on the terrace – it was a beautiful place to sit out with amazing views. When guests got out of their cars, they tended to stand transfixed. 'It's paradise,' they'd say.

We had a row of cypresses going down the hill to the pool, marking the edge of our property. On the west side of the house the ground fell away sharply and was covered with the olive trees. We also built what we called the Great Wall of China behind the house – a stone containing wall because the house was on such a steep hillside. We did it ourselves; I was mostly the cement mixer. The vegetable garden needed a lot of watering in the summer, it was so dry, but my herb garden flourished. In the winter, Peter and I were often on our own but come, Easter the children and friends started coming and I was very busy in the kitchen. We impressed some American guests by telling them that the mayonnaise was home-made with our own olive oil and eggs.

There were one or two other ex-pats living near us, some rather a disaster and quite a few who would hand out dud cheques and then buzz off. One couple invited us for dinner and the mother-in-law was there. 'Oh Silvia,' she said, 'You must join the English Club – we have our weekly order from Sainsbury's.' That was the last thing I wanted to do.

Our nearest town was Arezzo where there was a series of lovely frescos by Piero della Francesca and many people came to see them. There was a fresco in our village, too, and the head of the British School in Rome used to send his students there. When I heard about this, we invited him to tea. He came with a chauffeur and I had to give him (the chauffeur) a separate table and piece of cake. It was very embarrassing and the only time I have ever had to do anything like that. Maybe it was what the British School demanded. The head then invited us to the school in Rome to see if I remembered anything about it, but I had left when I was three, and I didn't.

The only thing that was really disastrous in the village was the bread and I always made my own, but I really appreciated all the lovely raw materials available. Our area in Umbria was very good for truffles and I could buy delicious truffle oil. Our village had only one shop and we got very friendly with the owners and with the owners of a family restaurant – they always had eight courses and you had to work your way through them. Every summer, each village had a *fiesta* with their own speciality food. One would have a polenta festival, another lamb, or zucchini. Our village had polenta and you had various places selling it with different sauces. They danced a lot, old-fashioned ballroom dancing, and one day we were watching this in the piazza when a guy came and grabbed me and took me off for the most dizzy, whirlwind dance I've ever experienced.

We had a campervan and when we bought it, one of the children said: 'Mum, why did you buy that, you'll never go anywhere.' It was a bit like that, but we did go to music festivals and to Florence, Orvieto and Assisi. There was an earthquake in Assisi though we weren't in the place when it happened; the cupola in the amazing church there fell and broke into pieces. It took a long time to rebuild it. It's a very earthquake-prone area.

At one time we decided to take B&B visitors to help with the financial situation. We had two apartments, one downstairs, one upstairs or they could have the whole house. It was a lot of work – eleven beds to make, sheets to wash, which I did. We had found a nice agency who sent us people and they'd say it was OK for us to take a week out every now and then for the family, we should just let them know. After a couple of years we were taking so many weeks out for the family that the agency said it wasn't for them any more.

We once had some Americans who had come on a sketching holiday. Both the women fell in love with the round table Bernard had bought all those years ago in the First World War, and when they came back the following year they told us they'd each bought a round table just like ours.

We had one family of five sisters who wanted a reunion. They said they hadn't seen each other for a long time but they were horrible to one of them. We once found her sleeping on our front door step and another time they chased her off down the drive shouting, 'Go, go away.' It was terrible.

Stephen Pritchard, *The Observer* music critic, and his wife came to stay and became close friends. They liked the house so much they wanted to buy it but it was just at the time we were thinking of leaving and they didn't want to come for three years. They managed to find a site they liked and it was almost next door to ours. It was practically a ruin and we used to go there to pick mushrooms. This was a truffle area too. When we returned to England and wanted to go back to Italy, we used to stay with them and they'd come to us in Ringmer when going to Glyndebourne.

Chapter 26

Sicily. I save a drowning man. After fourteen years in Italy, we return home. Mafia-type house agent. We take him to court. England. New opera house at Glyndebourne.

One year we thought we'd go to Sicily – I think the *Guardian* was doing a package holiday there. There were about a dozen of us in the group and one day after lunch, our guide suggested we might like to go down to the beach for an hour. We were wandering along the shingle and I was thinking about going for a swim – it was a lovely shallow, shelving beach – but I didn't have a costume or a towel. I saw an elderly woman sitting on the rocks and then noticed someone in the sea was waving. The elderly lady came up to me and said she thought her husband was in difficulties but I said, 'no, I think he's just waving'. Then I remembered the Stevie Smith poem, '*Not Waving But Drowning*', when a drowning man's distressed thrashing in the water was mistaken for waving. The woman said, 'No, he is in difficulty.' He had turned on to his back and couldn't get on to his front to make any headway. He was getting swept right down the coast. So I just dropped my jeans and swam out to him.

The story is only interesting because of the way people reacted. There were two young boys fishing nearby, and maybe they couldn't swim but they didn't do anything. A lot of people in my group retreated to the back of the beach. Peter said afterwards he was flabbergasted that I could take my jeans off so quickly. By the time I got to the man, he was unconscious and going rather blue. I managed to get him near the shore – it wasn't difficult because he *was* unconscious. I'd been taught life-saving and I remembered the instructor saying it's easier if a person is unconscious. They're in the water, they don't have weight and they're not fighting you. If conscious, they often try to resist. But as I got near the shore, he became very heavy – he was a big man and a dead weight – and I couldn't get him out of the water. The young chaps came and helped drag him on to the beach. He was blue, his eyes were closed, but no one else arrived. Then his wife came and I said I needed a towel and some dry clothes. They always tell you to wrap a person in a warm blanket, (from where? I wondered). I did all this, rubbed his limbs and he opened his eyes. The wife came back with a little towel and a spare pair of underpants and handed them to me which I thought was a bit strange. I had to strip off his wet pants and put the dry ones on and she stood by and let me do it. Funny, isn't it? I'm so glad I reacted as I did. You don't know, do you, how you'd act until something like that happens.

The tour leader took the man to hospital and the wife was very grateful. I think he was, too, but also embarrassed because, I afterwards discovered, I was a bit older than he was. One of the group invited us out to lunch, and one brought me some flowers.

It turned out that they were Mr. and Mrs Chase, the owners of Tyrrell's Potato Crisps, and had a large potato farm near the Welsh border. They sent me a lovely box of organic liquors and said that if any time we were passing we should come and see over their factory. I think their son runs it now and they've produced some marmalade vodka from the potatoes which they sell at £40 a bottle.

We'd been away from England for fourteen years and had the feeling it was time to go back. Peter was not very well. But the children loved the house. Paul and his wife usually came twice a year, and they were desperate when they knew we were going to sell it. 'Where can we go for our holidays?' they asked. We had thought of seeing if the children wanted to buy it, but that sort of thing can be difficult to organise and lead to quarrels. It was interesting that Peter and I both felt it was time to leave. No tears.

It was when we started planning to come home that we began having trouble with an Italian estate agent. When money is involved, the Italians have no holds barred. We had put the house on the market and had a call from an agent in Citta di Castello. He said he'd heard we were selling and he had many customers, Americans, who would pay a lot of money for it. 'Do come and see me in town,' he said.

I told him we already had three agents, but he said to come anyway. I was against it because he had once been to the house with some customers and looked a real Mafia type – dark glasses, the hat – and we didn't need him. But Peter decided to go and see him. It was a big town house and we went up to the first floor. His son was there, too.

The agent started talking and I suddenly came over feeling terribly unwell. I don't know what it was. The whole atmosphere of the place was weird. I said, "I'm terribly sorry but I'll have to go downstairs and wait on the street.' The atmosphere was just sinister. I went out and took some deep breaths and after a while they called me to go up to the office to sign something. I went up and said, 'I'm sorry, but I'm not signing anything.' And we left. But Peter had signed. He always thought everyone was nice. In the end we seemed totally in the thralls of this awful man. We had to go to court and only got out of the situation because I hadn't signed. We'd bought the house in both our names, so it took both of us to sign it out. In some marriages the man just signs and that's it. But we always did things together. We really felt we were being chased out of the country.

The agent we did have was really nice and very much on

our side. But it made a bad end to such a happy time. The woman who bought it had come with a girlfriend who was looking for a holiday home. She totally fell in love with it and said we shouldn't change anything, she'd have it just as it was. I said we'd have to take our books and furniture. Her husband never had time to come and must have bought it without seeing it. He said it was a tenth anniversary present for his wife.

Last days in Italy

Looking back on our time in Italy, it was a lovely, very positive way of life. I loved living in such a beautiful place, designing the house and garden, cooking, having friends and family to stay.

Chapter 27

Back to England. House-hunting. Ringmer. I create another garden. Peter dies. The funeral. Obituaries. Holiday in Kefalonia.

We came back to England in 2004 and had to look for somewhere to live. We'd thought of Sussex with all our Sussex connections: my granny who'd lived in Eastbourne, or Chailey, or Bath where our oldest son, Tobias, lived. But when Dominic, our youngest who lived in Ringmer, near Lewes, picked us up from the airport, he told us there were two houses for sale in his road. At that time Peter was having problems with his heart and we thought Ringmer was less hilly than Bath and the climate less muggy.

We planned to buy two bungalows but couldn't buy the one we liked most because the old lady who owned it had a daughter who had hoped to inherit it. In fact, the old lady left all her money to a dogs' home and the daughter contested the will which took so long, we just gave up. We bought the other house where an old man, a gun collector, had lived. The police had had to come every year to inspect his collection which he used to service in his shed.

We'd told the Italian company organising the move from Italy to bring a small van when they came to pack up everything, because the ground was very rough. But they brought an enormous one. It had just snowed so when they arrived they couldn't turn it round. We had to chop down one of our acacia trees for them to do it. I gave them pasta for lunch and they loaded up the van. Much of it didn't arrive for ages. When it did come, all my plants were missing, and my lemon tree. They never came. I think the company had changed carriers once or twice on the way.

We'd been away fourteen years and, actually, it was nice to be back. It was the sense of humour that struck me first. When someone delivers something here, they often have a joke with you. You don't get that in Italy. It was a little like getting into an old pair of shoes and we converted our new house very successfully to how we wanted it.

The shape of the garden was already there but nothing except brambles and two old apple trees. We had to get a lorry to come over the school playing fields next door to take the brambles away. I think the house, as in Italy, makes me feel like being in High and Over. My taste was definitely influenced by that light open plan in the sitting room, nothing very expensive but a nice mixture of old and new.

It was when we were away that the new Glyndebourne opera house had been built. We were sad in a way because our whole life had been bound up in the old building. But I could see their point. I thought it was marvellous that George Christie raised all that money and the architecture is lovely – I love it all being with such beautiful wood, it's like a sounding board and has very good acoustics. It's a pity about the fly-tower but what can you do, you have to have one. The old dining room has been much smartened up; it used to be where we rehearsed. At that time, there was a tree growing up through the middle and when we were trying to rehearse the ballet, it was rather awkward.

I don't think Peter got any more productions when we were back, perhaps one or two in Italy and Germany. He did *Falstaff* in Hanover with our son, Charles, as assistant producer, and his little grandson had a part in the first scene. Peter was in his nineties but very fit. We'd moved endlessly and I think he was very happy being in Ringmer. We had eight years here together and did a lot of nice things – we used to go up to London, to exhibitions, to the theatre, to Glyndebourne, the family came to visit us. When we were all here together, there was always so much laughter and Peter just enjoyed sitting at our big round table with the children even though, at the end, he wasn't quite understanding what was going on.

He died on Christmas Day 2012 and all the family came from many parts of the world for the funeral. I chose the music and Mark, who had come from Australia, and Margaret Constable, a lady from the village and one of the church wardens, helped me. Some of it was from *Orfeo*, the opera Peter had been working on when we'd first met in 1947, sixty-five years since I first started at Glyndebourne, and music we had loved together. Six of the children carried Peter's rush coffin. Theatre people who'd become friends came, and colleagues from the many opera companies he'd worked with.

He is buried in Ringmer. At the funeral, the undertaker hadn't dug the grave deep enough and we all had to go away and come back. I think perhaps the rush coffin took up more space than an ordinary one would have done. The company afterwards offered me a reduction on the gravestone. We now have a lovely dark slate, very plain with an inscription, but we didn't make it clear to the stone mason to leave room for me, so I think I'll have to go on the back. I don't know what's going to happen, but I won't have to deal with that, will I?

Peter had done so much for opera and been through many stressful times. As well as his productions in Glyndebourne and Germany, he had directed over fifty productions for Scottish Opera and was awarded an Honorary Doctorate for Services to Music by St. Andrew's University. He'd staged sixteen operas for the Wexford Festival and worked in America, Canada, South Africa, Italy, Denmark, Switzerland and France. He ran the Opera School in Toronto University for eighteen months.

There were obituaries in many national papers: *The Scotsman* wrote: 'from the outset he was an inspiring figure and as director of productions from 1965 to 1975, he was responsible for a wide variety of operas which included works by Monteverdi to *Don Pasquale* and *Fidelio.* He created Scottish Opera's first orchestra and staged the first ever *Ring Cycle* and *The Trojans* with Janet Baker in 1971 and 1972. He took opera to the Edinburgh Playhouse Theatre where audiences were the biggest ever for an opera in Scotland.'

It was very stressful at the end of Peter's life and after his death I found being by myself quite a rest. I did a lot of gardening, and then I thought I'd go to Kefalonia, on my own, be enterprising. But when I arrived, it was 40 degrees and I suddenly felt very dizzy and just fell flat. The hotel was very sweet but I had to go to hospital and Saga, the company I was with, wasn't able to wait for me to go on to the next place. My family decided Jessica should come out and rescue me and we had a lovely time together. She hired a car and we did lots of trips. I was still feeling a bit dizzy, and since then I've had the same thing in Ringmer. Nobody seemed to know what it was. The doctors said there were so many reasons why old people became dizzy. It did get better after a few months and Jessica and I decided we'd go back to Kefalonia to wipe out the bad memory. This time it was a feast of colours and the temperature was perfect.

Chapter 28

Memories

Memories

I am quite content with the way things are, very happy with my children and seeing all seventeen grandchildren developing, remembering having my babies all those years ago when we didn't have a washing machine until our sixth child, or a fridge for many years. In the London fogs (pea soupers), the nappies dried black and greasy with soot and that was indoors! 1953, I think. Sometimes, I washed them in the Glyndebourne dressing-room sink, and once nursed Tobias in my full *Macbeth* witches make-up.

I think I've passed on my parents' healthy eating habits to my children. Most of them have the same in spite of marrying wives who sometimes have quite different tastes! They're nearly all cooks, boys and girls, and a lot are gardeners, too. It's nice when these things are carried on. So many things have made me happy: sixty-one years of a strong marriage, eight well-balanced kids with good marriages, two step-daughters, long hikes with various daughters and Peter (the Welsh coast, South Downs Way, Scotland, the Cornish Way, the Coast to Coast), building the house in the Sedlescombe vineyard, rescuing the drowning man in Sicily, creating gardens, cooking, and most importantly, making homes for the family with much love and much laughter.

Chapter 29

Silvia (then Ashmole) at Glyndebourne. GF=
Glyndebourne Festival; EF= Edinburgh Festival.

1947/GF
Orfeo – Choreographer: Rupert Doone

Dancers:	**Silvia Ashmole**	Marion Bardas
	Betty Cooper	Judy Gold
	Anna Lendrum	Gillian Lowe
	Enid Martin	Betty Oglethorpe
	Yvonne Olena	Peggy Sager (soloist)
	Meeta Thomas	Audrey Turner
	Denis Carey	David Gill
	Barry Grantham	John Gregory
	John Paget	Colin Patrick
	Gordon Williams	Paul Hammond (soloist, a ballet master)

1952/GF
La Cenerentola – Choreographer: Pauline Grant

Dancers:	**Silvia Ashmole**	Irene Claire
	Anne Fairstone	Joanna Williams

Idomeneo and *Macbeth* – Choreographer: Pauline Grant

Dancers:	**Silvia Ashmole**	Irene Claire
	Anne Fairstone	Joanna Williams
	Michael Bayston	Nigel Burke
	Robert Harrold	

1953/GF

Alceste – Choreographer: Pauline Grant
La Cenerentola – Choreographer: Pauline Grant
Dancers: Joyce Hartwell   Anne Anderson
           Silvia Ashmole   Eileen Elton
           Anne Fairstone   Carole Greer
           Margaret Kovac   Mary Preston
           Nigel Burke (ass. to Grant)
           Michael Bayston
           Robert Harrold   Kenneth Smith

1953/EF

The Rake's Progress and *Idomeneo* – Choreographer:
Pauline Grant
Dancers: **Silvia Ashmole**   Anne Fairston
           Carole Greer   Margaret Kovac
           Michael Bayston   Nigel Burke
           Robert Harrold

La Cenerentola – Choreographer: Pauline Grant
Dancers: **Silvia Ashmole**,   Anne Fairstone,
           Carole Greer,   Margaret Kovac

1954/GF

Arlecchino – No choreographer credited
Don Giovanni – No choreographer credited
The Rake's Progress – Choreographer: Pauline Grant
Alceste – Choreographer: Pauline Grant assisted by Joyce
Hartwell
Dancers: Anne Anderson   **Silvia Ashmole**
           Yvonne Barnes   Anne Fairston
           Carole Greer   Anne Hyde
           Gay Owen   Anne Southwood
           Michael Bayston   David Gilbert
           Robert Harrold   David Reynolds

122

1954/EF

Le Comte Ory – Choreographer: Pauline Grant

Dancers:	**Silvia Ashmole**	Anne Fairston
	Anne Southwood	Michael Bayston

1956/GF

Idomeneo, Le nozze di Figaro and *Don Giovanni* –
Choreographer: Pauline Grant

Dancers:	Silvia **Ashmole**	Ann Edgar
	Dorothy Fraser	Margaret Pollen
	Margaret Thole	Sally Williams
	Harry Cordwell	Peter Scott
	Frederick Navarre	

1957/GF

Falstaff – Choreographer: David Ellis (By arrangement
with the Ballet Rambert)

Dancers:	**Silvia Ashmole**	Valerie Boulton
	Sally Chesterton	Anna Dimitrievitch
	Ann Price	Nora Ryan
	Joanna Seddon	Anne Winrow

1958/PA

Falstaff – Choreographer: David Ellis (By arrangement
with Ballet Rambert)

Dancers:	The Ballet Rambert	
	Sheila Alletson	**Silvia Ashmole**
	Shirley Dixon	Jennifer Dodd
	Carolyn Fey	Jennifer Kelly
	Thelma Litster	Valerie Marsh
	Gillian Martlew	Elsa Recagno
	June Sandbrook	Sylvia Singleton
	John Benfield	John Chesworth
	Norman Dixon	Norman Morrice

1959/GF

Idomeneo, La Cenerentola, Le Nozze di Figaro –
Choreographer: Robert Harrold

Dancers:	Silvia **Ashmole**	Molly Kenny
	Olga Petro	Sandra Powell
	Priscilla Pritchard	Oenone Talbot
	Pauline Drewett	Robert Harrold

1960/GF

Falstaff, Don Giovann, La Cenerentola – Choreographer:
Robert Harrold

Dancers:	**Silvia Ashmole**	Sally Chesterton
	David Eavis	Leda Harris
	Peter Hook	Shirley Macpherson
	Lesley Searle	Oenone Talbot
	Gabor Tokay	Anthony Wilson
	Fleur Woolley	

1960/EF

Arlecchino – Choreographer: Pauline Grant
Silvia Ashmole playing the role of Annunziata (Mute)

1963/GF

Le nozze di Figaro – Choreographer: Robert Harrold

Dancers:	**Silvia Ashmole**,	Oenone Talbot,
	Robert Harrold	

1964/GF

Macbeth – Choreographer: Pauline Grant

Dancers:	Valerie Deakin	**Silvia Ashmole**
	Maureen Feehley	Joy Frank
	Joanna Grant	Sandra Jack
	Isobel Metcalf	Priscilla Pritchard
	Christian Peters	Robin Willett

Chapter 30

What the children say

TOBIAS

I was born in 1952 and for most of my early life we lived in Germany (in Hannover and Düsseldorf), coming over to England in the summer months so that Dad and Mum could work at Glyndebourne. It meant that we went to many different schools in both Germany and England, but I didn't know that that was unusual at the time, and looking back on it now, I think it was a good thing to experience two different cultures and learn two different languages. I had a very happy childhood. We were a large and expanding family and there was always something to do. I enjoyed all the moving about and our 'exotic' foreign holidays to France.

I spent one year in a boarding school in Oxford, which I didn't enjoy, and then the family moved to Sussex, near Glyndebourne. I and my two next brothers went to the grammar school in Lewes. I enjoyed that, too, although, with all the getting there and coming back, it felt like weekdays were filled up with breakfast, going to school, being at school, coming back, tea, homework, bed and not much else. Also, we lived in quite an isolated place, so I suppose in retrospect we didn't have many friends outside the family but, of course the family was large enough to compensate!

For the last year of my schooling, Charles and I lived on a farm in Rodmell, as the rest of the family had gone to live in Germany permanently. That was a very interesting time, being with the farm family, catching rabbits with ferrets, herding cows, driving the Land Rover etc. The farmer's wife was a bit strict, but the couple were both kind at heart and we got on well with their children. I met an old friend, Murray, again recently in Ringmer.

After school, I spent a year living in Birmingham. This was because between taking my 'O' levels and 'A' levels I had changed my mind about what I wanted to study (from German to Politics) and where I wanted to study (Lancaster rather than Bangor). I got a job in an insurance company to use up the year between applying to university again – my first experience of paid work. Nice people but my first experience of casual racism; Birmingham had a lot of Indian and Pakistani immigrants and some of the white people in the office didn't like that fact.

The following year I finally went to Lancaster University, where I had four happy years. I very much enjoyed the learning, the socialising.....I was quite surprised that the government would actually pay you to have such a great time! I had some very good friends there which lasted for some time afterwards.

During and just after uni, I went on two trips overland to India, mind-blowing experiences. I had never realised before the huge differences in people's material situation but their basically similar hopes and fears/outlook on life. All the countries I went through were strange and exotic in different ways...it was an amazing experience. It also confirmed my left-wing political views – seeing so many peoples' lives blighted by unnecessary poverty, cruelty and injustice.

I lived in various parts of north London after that, doing temporary factory and caretaking work to save up for a holiday in Morocco, and then office work for local councils. And I did voluntary work for the Advisory Service for Squatters, helping homeless people squat empty properties. But I couldn't find paid work that I enjoyed. I decided to retrain; I had fancied carpentry but the only course that started straight away was computer programming so I did that instead.

I found the course quite interesting in a dry, academic kind of way but didn't think it would suit me as a career, but I remember thinking that teaching a course like that would interest me. A few weeks after finishing the course, the college offered me a job teaching younger students office and work skills.

Although it was stressful, I really enjoyed being a teacher especially for students having a 'second chance' at education. But best of all, this was where I met my wife, Pam, who was a careers advisor at the same college. We met in the autumn of 1984 and I was bowled over by meeting my soul-mate at last. We married six months later – happiest day of my life – and I also became stepfather to my children Kerry (15 at the time) and Tom (10 years old). I felt my life began again at that moment and since then – 32 years ago – life has been full of the joys of sharing my life with Pam. We are rarely separated, are incredibly proud of our children and dote on our grandchildren! We love our organic gardening, are practising Buddhists and busy members of the local Labour Party.

As time has gone on, we have moved westwards: to Newbury in Berkshire, to Oxfordshire, to Bath and now to North Devon. And I have changed my job from teaching computing, to being an actual computer programmer. Latterly, I was able to work from home.

Now I am retired and we are busier than ever!

CHARLES

I was born in Woolwich on March 24th 1953 and spent the first years of my life in various homes with my parents as they often moved house. I have almost no memories of these homes or the first schools we attended – there were simply too many. Things calmed down a bit when Ades became the family home and I went to boarding school at Oxford with Tobias. I can't say I was particularly happy there and a spate of sleepwalking was probably a sign of that. It was nice to have the grandparents at Iffley, whom we could visit on Sundays, and they took us on trips on the river in the punt or canoe, and they had a wonderful garden for playing or roaming around.

After boarding school I went to Lewes County Grammar School for Boys which amalgamated with the girls' equivalent when I reached sixth form. Here I made friends with classmates for the first time (before this the stay at each school was so short that there was no time for a long-term friendship). For these years I lived first with a family my parents had found halfway to Seaford because my family was going to move to Germany, then, for my final year, with a teacher from school, whose two eldest daughters had moved out.

Living on the farm at Southease was fun because we did things, we had had no chance to do before (driving a Landrover across the fields . . .) but I did not find the mother very sympathetic. The teacher, who was renowned as being very strict, was a great person and had a sweet wife, both of whom were very interested in music and opera (!) so we got on very well.

Next stop was Glasgow university where I did a combined Honours course in Drama and German. This was the first time anyone had taken this combination (usually the Drama students had English as second subject, or Fine Art) so the two departments had to sort that out. I enjoyed my time there immensely, living partly in a student hall and partly in a flat with fellow students. As part of my German course I was to do a stint in Germany to perfect the use of the language and I managed to reduce the expected full year to six months on the grounds that my German was so good! My father gave me the opportunity to work at the theatre where he was *Intendant,* Bielefeld town theatre. This is where my future wife, Conni, saw me for the first time, as I jumped from the first circle onto stage as part of the performance I was acting in, and gave her quite a fright as she was sitting very close by.

After finishing university a year later I got a job at the same theatre again, although the *Intendant* was now someone else, and was introduced to Conni officially. We went to Bonn, where I had my next job and Conni went into teacher training and from there we moved to Hannover in 1980. That summer we married in Glasgow, where my parents lived in Kirklee Gardens.

We have lived in or near Hannover ever since and celebrated the births of our children, Jan in 1982 and Sarah in 1984. I was fortunate in that the *Intendant* in Hannover, Peter Lehmann, knew me since I was a child, as he had been assistant to Carl and so knew Glyndebourne et al. Mr Lehmann's biggest interest was in the works of Richard Wagner, so I was lucky again in having had quite a bit of experience at the Bayreuth Festival (on and off since 1973). He supported me whenever I wanted to go to the festival for work again in the summer, which meant getting special leave, and remained my boss till he retired in 2001. I was occasionally given the opportunity to do a production of my own, but usually assisted the director in his work. Any revival, I felt, I was entitled to "improve" in the details and that was always fun. The most longstanding production I was looking after was a production of *Hänsel and Gretel* which had opened in 1964! It was revived each year for about ten performances around Christmas (the operatic equivalent of the pantomime!). In the course of the years I have 'built in' countless singers in the various roles and had a ball 'improving' details all the time – it is amazing how even after 20 years a detail may catch your eye and you think: we should change that!

Another highlight was the production of *Der Freischütz*
we did in Vietnam with a completely Vietnamese cast,
always working through an interpreter. It was interesting
to see where the cultural diffences became apparent: the
older people in the chorus did not want to kneel to the
young singer doing the 'Monk' (old people are highly
revered there), and a simple peasant waltz was something
they had no idea about. Even pairing off: one boy dances
with one girl had to be "enforced"! The people were
wonderful though, the conditions quite different from
Germany, of course. The city of Hanoi with its intriguing
old town and the surrounding countryside was an
incredible experience. (I was lucky to have done this,
because years later a course of tuition with Korean
students was initiated in Hannover and again I worked
with an interpreter to explain what was wanted.)

There was a bit of a crisis in the following five years in
Hannover as the new *Intendant* tried out new forms of
staging and some ultra-modern pieces, which did not meet
the audiences' taste. Since 2006 Dr Klügl has been in
charge and he has found a balance between modernity and
'classic' opera/theatre which was accepted by the
audiences and the critics alike!

So there were good times and rough times at the theatre,
but I loved the job and enjoyed working with almost
everyone involved until about two years ago, I realised I
was almost constantly unhappy with the concepts
presented or did not agree with the way the directors were
rehearsing and decided to go into retirement in the summer
of 2017.

In the autumn of 2016 the idea was launched in the family
that we could move into a house together with our
daughter and her family (she had moved back to Hannover

and had two children) so my final nine months at the theatre were running parallel to finding, buying and renovating our new home, which we have now moved in to and are enjoying to the full, including looking after the grandchildren.

Cooking! Important theme. Had always enjoyed cooking with Mum and was obviously influenced by her likes and dislikes. The boom of TV programmes about cooking did not pass me by – I tended to watch one in the afternoon, recovering from the morning rehearsal. I decided I could cook as well as the candidates on TV could, and applied to take part. And blow me, they took me! Six candidates cook a dish of their own, starting on Monday, every day one candidate was evicted. Leaving two on Friday to cook dishes prescribed by the conferencier-cook. I got through to Friday but lost the final (partly because I rarely made mayonnaise and never custard (reminder of school food). But despite losing, it was a great time and the experience spurred me on to improve what I knew about cooking and awakened a desire to try out as many techniques as possible.

A few years later I was contacted with the offer to take part in a completely new show, which was based on a different idea. Who is the better cook? Man or woman? Two teams of two competed by creating a three-course meal out of a set of given ingredients. Basics like eggs, oil, flour etc were always available. But no spices unless they were among the twelve additional ingredients. But we could 'earn' ourselves three additional ingredients by answering quiz-questions during the show. The cooking time was forty minutes, so no chance to backtrack much. I asked Paul to join me as a team and we marched through the whole thing (4 programmes) beating all the girls' teams that we were pitted against. Very good fun, but nerve-racking. Conni was at her wit's end because Sarah was taking her final exams at university the same day as we did the final cooking challenge! We all came through with flying colours.

It was always good having siblings around to play/do things with because friends were unheard of in my early childhood. And it is great fun now seeing everyone (including the next generation, of course) when we have a family reunion. In general we seem to get on quite well with each other although the amount of contact obviously varies. We hope family will come and visit us in our new home if they are passing by.

PAUL

Hello, I'm Paul, third in line and born on 2nd September 1955 in London (although the family was already living in Germany, I believe in Berlin).

The first few years we spent in Hannover and then in Düsseldorf, where I started my schooling at the army primary school. I remember a holiday to Switzerland I had with both parents alone (the school had to close due to some epidemic), which was very unusual. We moved to England where I visited various schools and then went to Christ Church Cathedral School in Oxford. The highlights were Sundays, when I walked along the towpath to my grandparents' house and had exciting, busy and interesting times with Bernard, my grandfather, and lovely food cooked by granny. After that, I went to the Grammar School in Lewes for a year with Tobias and Charles before moving to Augsburg in 1968. We had to walk from our house in Chailey about a mile to get the bus into Lewes and I was very proud going with my big brothers. We had lots of fun in the big garden playing with the other children from the houses next door.

In Germany, I had a tough time at the very academic school, doing classics, in Augsburg but when we moved to

Bielefeld the standards were a lot lower, so I got on really well. In 1977, after a very colourful schooling life, I took my *'Abitur'*, the A-level equivalent, in Bielefeld. A year before, I met Barbara at school, who later became my wife. We both studied in Münster, a well-known university town fairly near by, where I studied medicine and Barbara qualified as a primary school teacher.

Barbara and I got married in 1982 and moved back to Bielefeld in 1984. I started work at one of the hospitals (and after six months at another) doing a five year specialization in gynaecology and obstetrics. During this period our daughter, Jennifer, was born in 1986 and our son Christopher four years later in 1990. Barbara was working at different primary schools in and around Bielefeld, taking time out after the children were born.

In 1990 I spent 15 months in Hamburg in a well-known clinic for IVF treatment and endocrinology, where I acquired this additional qualification. This turned out to be the best and most important decision in my working life.

Ten years after I started a oprxis for gynaecology and obstetrics in 1991, a colleague and I additionally founded an IVF clinic, which has steadily grown since then giving us great satisfaction in helping young couples achieve their greatest wish of becoming parents.

Jennifer and Christopher are lovely children, very different but both sweet. They both started school at the British Army school in Bielefeld, Jennifer then went to Bedgebury boarding school in Kent, while Christopher spent the last years at school at Hilton College in South Africa with his cousins (Andrea's sons). We regularly spent the summer holidays in Italy with Peter and Silvia and to this day the children remember these holidays with great joy. Jennifer has since done a degree in International Business at Bristol University and went on to qualify as an accountant,

133

working in the finance departments in hospitals in Sussex and then in London. This last year she quit her job and is currently just finishing an MBA course in Cambridge, which she vastly enjoyed. Christopher also went into medicine and after studying in Hannover qualified as a doctor in 2016. He is currently working and specializing in a hospital in Arnsberg, also doing gynaecology and obstetrics. He has a very sweet fiancee and is planning to get married next year. Barbara is still working and very much enjoying teaching at a primary school in Bielefeld where, I am sure, she does a fantastic job.

In our spare time we both love to travel, cook, garden, participate in our children's lives and golf (that's more me than Barbara!)

JESSICA

Even when I was young I remember feeling somehow 'different'. When we were out and about our large family always seemed to catch peoples' attention. And my friends were always keen to take part in the fun. But at home, it was all I knew and nothing different. And it was fun. Today I am even more appreciative of having so many siblings. The support they give in good times and bad. I remember helping a lot with the daily peeling of potatoes for ten hungry people and running along next to Silvia when out shopping, as she was quite a busy mother. And always full of energy and positive thinking. These qualities helped her with dealing with her day-to-day routine. And her very loving, open and friendly mind.

I was born on the 10th January 1958 (same birthday as Andrea!) in Hanover, Germany, where Peter and Silvia happenend to be living at the time. Silvia wasn't amused by the midwife saying she must see how much **it** weighs as ‚girl' in German carries the neuter (case): "*Das Mädchen*". After giving birth to three boys she was looking forward to some promising female company.

A happy childhood spent in Sussex came to an abrupt end when the family yet again uprooted itself to move to Augsburg in Germany. I inherited some talent for dancing and danced professionally for 12 years, working with a number of choreographers in various towns in Germany, perpetuating the gypsy life style I had become accustomed to.

By the time I was 30 years old, I and my Welsh/Australian husband Rhys, also in the theatre, had moved to Berlin, a city that fascinated us. Here we settled in a flat on the Eastern border of Western Europe, one year before the fall of the Iron Curtain and haven't moved since. Blessed with two daughters, Rebecca and Zoë, and a step-daughter Jacintha, and overjoyed with motherhood, I decided, once the children were old enough, to pursue another calling or passion, and opened a bookshop. It sells both German and English literature and is located just around the corner from where I live, in a neighbourhood where many people with nomadic life-styles from all over the world seem to gather and find their harbour. The blend of cultures never ceases to fascinate me and maybe this is why I, coming from quite a blend myself, can call the city my home.

ANDREA (ANDY)

I was born on my sister Jessica's second birthday and the fifth of Silvia and Peter's children. Our idyllic childhood in Chailey, Sussex, meant I could spend my days roaming around on the neighbour's farm herding cattle, playing hide and seek in the straw barn and generally loving the freedom of rural life. Once the family moved to Germany when I was eight, learning German was our first challenge in order to make friends at school and to fit in with our peer groups. I pursued my love of gymnastics with a local club and progressed from there to ballet school, following my big sister's lead. She and I became very close, living away from home in a boarding school for ballet scholars in Stuttgart and where I managed to bow out of really making an effort, academically. Our afternoons were filled with classes, or sewing point shoe ribbons, knitting leg warmers or doing our own washing – school homework took a back seat. I loved our years in Stuttgart with the wonderful friendships growing out of being thrown together with people from all parts of the world wanting to be part of the renowned ballet company. We worked very hard and became incredibly fit but I grew very tall and developed problems with my knees necessitating me to take six months off for my bone structure, to catch up with the exercise I had been taking.

I moved to Glasgow where my parents and younger siblings had moved to and was persuaded to use my 'down time' to learn useful crafts like driving, typing and other secretarial skills, while also keeping fit by swimming daily, in readiness for my return to Stuttgart to finish my dance tuition. I had discovered life 'on the outside' and realised quite how wrapped up we had become in following our dream of dancing, without taking a moment to live life as teenagers. I yearned to leave Germany and at eighteen, I returned to Glasgow where I worked at Scottish Opera for a few years, having injured my ankle in a fall and rather given up the dancing dream. Scotland is such a peaceful and beautiful country and I embraced all it had to offer – exploring the Highlands and Lochs at weekends. My younger brother Mark was attending Glasgow University at the time and so we lived together in a flat as Mum and Dad had in the meantime returned to Sussex to follow their idea of becoming an opera director /assistant team wherever in the world this took them.

I met my future husband, Harry while working for him in his sport and leisurewear business in Brighton. We married seven years later and settled in Sussex on a forty acre farm which became our haven for bringing up our four children, Olly, Jack, Max and Cassie. We had a flock of two hundred sheep, golden retriever dogs whom we took great delight in training as gun dogs, and a country lifestyle that fitted around Harry's workaholic days. In 2000, I miraculously managed to haul Harry out of his office for six months and we undertook a Motorhome adventure throughout the US with the four children. This was a life changing experience for us and more importantly one that opened our eyes to the world.

By 2002, we had sold up in Sussex and moved lock, stock and family to the north-eastern corner of South Africa, where we discovered an eclectic community of fantastic people who had got out of the Johannesburg/Cape Town rat race and were bringing up their children in the magical surroundings of Mpumalanga. Harry and I learnt to fly small airplanes. I followed my love of natural medicine and qualified as a homeopath. I did some volunteer work and we bought a small timber plantation and built our dream home. But most importantly, we educated our children at incredible schools from which they emerged as fit and sporty, confident, grounded and well-rounded young people with qualifications to gain entry into any UK university of their choice. Every school holiday we would set off in our campervan or combi and explore the southern African continent for weeks or even months at a time. We never felt threatened or in danger although we had learnt to be aware of our surroundings and to be vigilant when out in 'the bush'.

Harry and I set off, with other pilots and their planes on many long exploration flights up the spectacular Mozambique coast line all the way to Zanzibar, to the historic Isla de Mozambique, Malawi, Zambia and of course numerous trips to neighbouring Botswana and the impressive Delta. Namibia, with its ever changing landscape of desert, mountains, gravel roads, coast line, wildlife and canyons, is an adventure in its own right, whether on a trekking holiday through the Fish River Canyon, visiting by car or by air. We never tired of our self-guided trips and experienced sights and sounds we would never forget.

Our eldest son, Olly, had just started his studies at Oxford when he collapsed and died of an undiagnosed heart disease, Cardiomyopathy, turning our world upside down within seconds. There was absolutely nothing anyone could do to help us with the shock and devastation so we gathered our children around us and dealt with the grief as best we could. There is an on-going sense of loss daily but I have had to learn to deal with the fact and ensure our children are not affected by my wish to over protect them. One by one they left South Africa to study in the UK and a few years ago Harry and I, along with Cassie who was still at school, decided to return from South Africa as the security situation there was becoming more dangerous. Living on a farm was beginning to feel like a death sentence, one we weren't prepared to take.

We now spend our time between sunny Spain where we pursue our love of all things outdoor like Padel tennis, golf, walking, swimming and driving over to the Alps, where the fresh mountain air we missed for ten years, refreshes our minds. In the meantime, Jack lives and works in Singapore, Max in Vancouver and Cassie is at university in Leeds. They couldn't be further apart but our strong family bond remains intact and we love getting together on trips all around the world. We have travelled extensively with the family since they were small and still now manage to find corners of the world we are all keen to explore... the adventures continue.

We recently bought a forty bedroom hotel in Devon. Life with the Tuckers is never dull – we follow our interests and learn new skills leaving no stone unturned.

Mum and I are very similar in likes and dislikes, character and sense of humour, and once my children were born, I began to realise quite how much work and what sacrifices she and Dad made to ensure all of us had the education and upbringing they strived for. We siblings have all followed our chosen life paths with our parents' blessing and advice and more importantly unconditional love. It has been an incredible journey so far and I feel I have been very lucky to have had their input and example to follow.

MARK

We were living in Seaford at the time with Dad working at the Glyndebourne Festival Opera. Then on a dark and stormy night which caused a detour on the way to the hospital in Brighton, I arrived. 27 August 1962.

Peter and Silvia bought their first home, a subdivided part of Ades house, Chailey, later that year. Surrounded by siblings and neighbouring kids with garden and fields to explore, must have been fun.

In 1967 I started in the local school in Chailey – I remember my sister, Andy, pushing me into the flint stone wall which required a doctor's attendance and stitches to the back of my head.

In 1968 we moved to Augsburg in Germany where Peter started his first position as *"Intendant"*, the general manager of the theatre there. I started school again – in Germany, school starts when you are six years old. We lived in Goeggingen, a suburb of Augsburg. More fun places to explore and get up to things that were frowned upon. My friend Wolfgang's parents found out about us smoking cigarettes in the nearby woods and he was so severely beaten with a strap that he wasn't able to go to school for a week. For some reason, I thought that Silvia had also found out and decided smoking was to be avoided. I remember cycling around everywhere come hail wind or shine – this is probably where my love of cycling developed!

Holidays were always a big thing. I think my parents really made an effort to make them special whether it was the Norfolk broads, camping or Club Med on Corsica, or in Tunisia.

After that, moves to Bielefeld and Wiesbaden – spending as much time on my bike and as little as possible on schoolwork. Never motivated, always lazy, just scraping by with dismal marks. Trick number 1 was getting one of the parents to sign off on my abysmal schoolwork at seven in the morning before I went off to school.

I remember sitting in the kitchen in Wiesbaden when Peter announced that we would be moving to Glasgow. Oh shit. From being the Pom in Germany I went to being the Fritz in Scotland. Luckily we went to a private school – with an 800 year history no less, so bullying wasn't as bad as it could have been. But it did mean school uniforms for the first time since I was five. Awful. I was even pressured to shave by the physics teacher because I and another in the class were showing the first signs of a moustache! He was made to do it in front of the class – I was allowed to shave in the comfort of home. Not sure why.

I don't remember when I first went sailing – certainly I always liked boats – the holidays on the Norfolk Broads or steering a ferry on the Wolfgangsee in Austria. The sailing course/holiday in Scotland was a highlight – the parents and a few others went on a camping holiday and I had the treat of a sailing course. Particularly on the last day on my own mastering the main and the jib in good wind hanging over the side contemplating the centreboard – great fun and something I will never forget!

So Glasgow saw more trouble in school, but at least the German exams were easy!

After repeating some H-Grade classes while doing A-Levels in others in my last year, my grades were good enough for an entry to Mechanical Engineering at the University of Glasgow down the road. I'd always been interested in things mechanical – reading technical magazines and interested in cars from day one.

In Glasgow we had a TV! Wow! After not having had one all the time we were in Germany. What was that about? Started watching Formula 1 – which I do to this day – *The New Avengers* which scared me shitless as I had to turn the light off at the bottom of the stairs before climbing them to get to my second floor bedroom.

The weather in Glasgow was either appalling or bad – with very short interludes of pleasant. That didn't stop some people walking around in T-shirts with 5 C outside! A few months after I started at Glasgow uni, Bernard finished at Scottish Opera. After selling the five toilet/ten fireplace mansion, they bought a flat for Andy and myself and moved back to Ades in Sussex.

A few months after I started at Glasgow uni, I made some new friends, Jim and Dave in particular – and still had regular contact with my only school friend, Peter, who was a year above me and went to Edinburgh to study computing. I shared a flat with Jim and Dave, and had a lot of fun in the process, including a couple of parties where the police ended up being called!

Despite being introduced to drinking – first cider then beer – I managed to get thru Uni with a 2.1 Honours degree. A very theoretical course of which I only ever used a minor proportion in later life. Towards the end it was job applications including a urine test the day after my graduation and a colour test (the job was for an electricity authority). Without a job in sight in Scotland I moved back home to Ades and looked around there.

The smallest 1" x 1" advertisement in one of the newspapers turned out to be the industrial refrigeration division of Carrier Air Conditioning working out of a demountable next to the former distributor-now-office of the comfort cooling section. Learnt a lot in those three years (what is a "flange" anyway?) with the help of my boss, Bob.

I built a Dutton Phaeton kit car in a hurry – I was using the parents' Golf to get to work – in the draughty garage in what seemed to be the coldest winter ever. Great fun – both the build and hooning around Sussex. Still amazed that I (and others) survived!

In between was a year-long stint with a girl on the outskirts of London in Bromley where my cat disappeared. I'd promised my girl friend to go and live in Germany after that so I tendered my resignation and ended up still with Carrier in Hamburg as part of their attempt at industrial refrigeration.

I lived in Hamburg for 7 years – up to 1994 – and then met a kind, sexy, fun girl called Silke when I already had a visa to migrate to Australia. After a while she asked permission of her lovely Mum, Magda, whether she could follow me out. I left in May 1994 with Silke following in December when her divorce and visa had come thru. Magda, in the meantime was together with Otto, who was an old customer of hers at the bank and who pursued her until she gave in.

As a farewell holiday, we took a last minute trip to Isla Margarita off Venezuela. Apart from absolute poverty (it seems things haven't improved) which meant the resort was surrounded by a 2.5 m wall with armed guards at the gates. We met Bernd and Verena there. They're from just outside of Hamburg and we have been friends with them and go on frequent holidays together since then.

In Australia we settled in Marrickville, near my brother-in-law's sister Kay and her husband Bob, and have stayed in the suburb ever since, buying our house in 1995. Bob and Kay remain good friends to this day and we socialise with them regularly. Apart from Bob and Kay some of the first people we met were Ray and Georgette – both of Lebanese extraction who were our neighbours in our unit block in Marrickville and took us into their extended and loud family. Many Lebanese BBQ at both their and Ray's parents' homes.

On my arrival in Australia, it took a couple of months to find my first job – I guess recent migrants are at the bottom of the list when it comes to employment. But a small company in the north of Sydney gave me a chance. We made milk cooling equipment to an innovative design of the "mad inventor" partner in the business. Silke arrived on her prospective marriage visa and we got married in my boss's back yard on 21 January 1995.

After a year things weren't picking up with the milk cooling equipment sales and an opportunity came up to join Carrier again in the guise of their commercial-packed unit division APAC. After six weeks my boss, the branch manager, confided in me that he was leaving and that as far as he was concerned I should be the next to be in charge! Gulp! Somehow, and probably displaying how out of my depth I was, we managed to get thru until the entire division was merged with Carrier and we moved from our own office in Rosehill to Carrier's head office in Rozelle.

One of my highlights was always sailing. One year, the parents came out for Peter's 80th and we drove (God knows why), but I do like driving the 2,000 km to Airlie Beach where we hired a catamaran yacht and sailed around the Whitsundays for five days having a wonderful time. We had some funny experiences on the way, including Dad being given iced water without the water at a Pizza joint and Mum asking for cutlery at McDonalds.

Other the years we've travelled a bit around Australia: up to Cooktown in northern Queensland, Perth in WA, Darwin to Uluru in NT. Most of those holidays were with Bernd and Verena. Magda and Otto visited us regularly until they were unable to do so due to advancing age and we stepped up our visits back to Germany and England.

We're still in our little house in Marrickville. Apart from my passion in energy conservation, I do follow politics and despair at Australia's leadership in the last fifteen years, always hoping for improvement. Or a soft revolution! A climate change policy, for instance.

I work for a German company in commuter room air-conditioning which, funnily enough, has their head office very near where I used to live in Hamburg.

The funny thing about being in a big family is that we never actually all lived together in one place. By the time Dominic was born, Tobias and Charles had remained in school in England so it never happened. The only times we were all together were festive occasions and holidays.

It was always very special be around the 'big uns' when they were at home, or to share those holiday experiences – there are many and varied stories that have entered the family lore.

One of the interesting things about a big family is the spread of beliefs, characters and careers. For example, within the family we have a whole range of political opinions from one of the spectrum to the other! On more than one holiday, Mum did a good job of getting like minded-people to bunk together, making the whole occasion more harmonious.

SUSANNA

By the time I came along in 1964, my oldest brother was on the verge of becoming a teenager. The older boys and Dishi and Tabs went away to boarding school, an occurrence which became more marked when we moved to Augsburg, Germany and they stayed behind to finish their education in England. Later, Jessica and Andrea went off to boarding school in Stuttgart so, us three 'little ones' formed a more 'normal' family at home with Mum and Dad. The over-riding thing was that you were rarely on your own and, if you were, it was out of choice. Sharing everything was a given and siblings had a good way of putting you in your place if you got too big for your boots. Silvia made sure no-one was left out, in all matters she seemed to me to be as fair as it was possible to be. Holidays must have been massive logistical challenges, with people coming in from all over the place, often with friends tagging along. I always loved big family gatherings as you were never stuck for someone to play/discuss/argue with. Tobias and Charles were fascinating, their lives seemed so extraordinarily grown-up for little me and I particularly liked Tobias even though I probably didn't know him very well. He was always gentle and considerate, whereas Charles could be quite scary at times! Whatever the occasion, there was always much laughter, good-humoured teasing and talk. Despite being one of many, I always felt that Silvia managed to make each one of us special in some way and successfully accommodated our varied interests with after school activities and the like. I loved Ades, so much space for everyone, yet room to retreat if you needed quiet time. All the time we lived in Germany, my dream was to return to Ades, surely because of the happy time we had spent there.

Silvia was then and continues to be, the glue that kept the family together. No matter how far-flung we were, she was the pivotal rock with, so it seemed, solutions to every problem. One would imagine she must have been consumed by worry most of the time, especially once the older ones became more independent, but there was always a smile and nearly always a 'yes' to every question posed. I think the over-riding thing I learned was to try and agree, if at all possible, to my own children's requests. I think her outlook empowered a feeling of independence and self-preservation which has stood us in good stead. Whatever the challenges each one of us faced, there was always support in practical terms or just on the end of the phone – I remember Silvia trying unsuccessfully to send money to Tobias in India and making a sofa cover with another child after a traumatic boyfriend break-up. I also remember friends moaning about their mothers and thinking there was really nothing I could say – my mother was perfect just the way she was – loving, nurturing, challenging, intelligent, beautiful, committed, hard-working and a very difficult act to follow!

I was born in November 1964, destined to be a boy to play with Mark (by this time just over two years old). Instead, a very small, rather jaundiced girl appeared weighing only 7lb. As a child, I was rather quiet and shy with a keen interest in animals. Mark, myself and later Dominic were the three 'little ones' as the oldest children were already living away from home being educated in Britain or Germany, with the two girls at boarding school in Stuttgart.

I went to *kindergarten* in Augsburg and learnt to speak German before joining the local primary school. A little grey rabbit to look after and then a little mongrel dog satisfied the animal longings to some extent although horses featured large. In Wiesbaden, Mark and I started riding lessons at the local rather posh German riding school. The move to Scotland was quite an upheaval. Alpha, the dog, and the rabbit stayed behind in Germany and the private school uniform was not appreciated. For a child who lived in jeans, a skirt and tights were just horrible. The best thing about the school was the chance to make friends with other girls who were just as horse-mad, one of whom is still a good friend. After two years, the move to Sussex meant a promise of living in the country, lots of roaming the local rights of way and enjoying the woodland around the little lake.

A year between school and university learning about pony breeding was where I met my future partner, Chris. I studied Zoology and Psychology at Reading University, where Chris bought a little house so we could live together. The university was renowned for its agriculture courses and my research was on using different surfaces to prevent sows squashing their new-born piglets. We married in 1986, and lived upstairs at Ades until Peter and Silvia moved to Italy. I was working as an Editor on a small local country magazine and we moved to Handcross, West Sussex, where Caroline was born in 1990. Everyone was rather surprised when I announced I was pregnant, they thought I would be better off with a dog or pony. The locals all thought Caroline was bound to be born in the woods as I spent a lot of time walking there!

Alice followed in 1992, Sarah in 1994 and just after Lucy was born in 1996, Chris got a new job as Manager in heavy haulage at Stiller's in Darlington, County Durham. The move was completed in March 1997 and the girls soon acquired northern accents! I started working for Tumble Tots, a gymnastic programme for 1-7 year olds, and later trained as a teaching assistant. Soon after, I did a year's training to become a primary school teacher via the graduate training programme and have since worked as a supply teacher around North Yorkshire. Once the girls were a little older, we acquired an Exmoor pony and they all learnt to ride. I became the secretary of the Yorkshire Exmoor Pony Trust and now spend considerable chunks of time caring for eighteen ponies and co-ordinating the business of the charity. I have two ponies of my own and love living in the country with all this fabulous countryside around us.

DOMINIC

I was born on November 16, 1968, in Augsburg, Germany, the wee one that everyone loves. Lived in Germany and moved to Bielefeld and subsequently Wiesbaden before, aged nine, moving to Glasgow and then back to the family home in Sussex in 1980. On the first day of school in Lewes I was introduced to Nicky, who became my childhood sweetheart and who I would eventually marry in 1991. I've loved sharing the last 25 years with my soul-mate.

After falling into work at my brother-in-law's t-shirt business straight from school, we moved to Northants and back to Sussex as jobs changed. Staying in Sussex, I became a director in a couple of businesses and ran these for some years but these closed down. After Peter's death in late 2012, the family moved to our current home in Suffolk. We have four children, Sam (22) finishing a degree at the University of Brighton this summer, Rohan (18) finishing an engineering diploma at West Suffolk College. Christian (16) who's just finished his GCSEs and Poppy (14) who's just starting her GCSE courses, not forgetting our border terrier, Skye.

I enjoy sport (watching), tennis (playing until an elbow injury stopped that), films, camping, dog walks, family time. When the kids have finished their schooling we plan to move back nearer the sea and would love the opportunity to build our own house, possibly abroad?